Children of the East

The Spiritual Heritage of Islam in the Bible

James Appel, MD

**You can obtain additional copies of this book by visiting
www.createspace.com/3603603**

Front cover photo courtesy of Emily Wilkens

Rear cover photo courtesy of James Appel, MD

Author photo courtesy of Hannah Thomas

Cover design by James Appel, MD

Contact the author at ChildrenoftheEast@gmail.com

In memory of
Dr. Robert Darnell

Contents

Preface

I am not a Muslim. I don't know Arabic. I don't have a degree in Islamic Studies. I grew up as a conservative Christian who didn't eat pork, didn't smoke, didn't drink, didn't dance, didn't gamble, etc. etc. etc.

So what makes me qualified to write a book on Islam and Christianity? Nothing really. But I felt like I should anyway. I do have some personal experience. I've lived and worked with Muslims for the last seven years in the Republic of Chad. I've treated them in the hospital and clinic. I've operated on them. I've visited their villages and slept in their houses. They've slept in mine. We've eaten together, fasted together and feasted together.

Also, over the past five years I've read many books and been introduced to some audio tapes of talks about Islam and Christianity that have inspired me to think differently. I've started to seek to learn more about this great monotheistic religion claimed by a quarter of the world's population as their creed and way of life.

At least from the perspective of Islam in the Bible, I do have a little credibility. I was not only raised a Christian but got my undergraduate degree (BA) in Christian Theology. I've not only studied Christianity, though, but I've actually read the entire Bible at least once and many parts of it numerous times.

And even though I'm obviously not a Muslim scholar, I have read bits and pieces of the Qur'an over the last several years. Last year, during the month of Ramadan, I finally read it from cover to cover. While I haven't read it in Arabic, only the Meaning of the Qur'an in English, I do have some understanding of the book that founded the faith of Islam.

So while my profession is medicine and surgery, the practical arts of helping people and saving lives, my real passion is God and spirituality. And what I've learned about the spiritual heritage of Islam in the Bible is nothing less than astounding.

So, here we go...

Acknowledgments

To Dr. Robert Darnell whose four sermons at Loma Linda University Church that I heard on tape are the inspiration for this book.

To Stephen Dickie whose sermons and book inspired me to study more the commonalities between Islam and Christianity.

To Mahamat Saleh Abakar for inspiring me with what true Islamic faith can be, for our many enlightening discussions about God, may you rest in peace.

To Franklin Cobos for pointing me in the right direction so many times toward so many useful resources in my search for truth. Thanks for our many insightful discussions.

To Bryan Gallant for his sermons on the Children of the East which further inspired me to dig deeper on this subject.

To my parents, Jim and Gladys, who both started out skeptical that there really could be reconciliation between Christianity and Islam but have turned into my biggest allies and sounding boards.

To my Uncle Dan for his open mind, challenging questions and great book recommendations.

To the many authors who have guided me and opened my eyes without them even knowing it.

To Karen Armstrong for her wonderful book *Muhammad*.

To Mark Siljander for his eye-opening book *A Deadly Misunderstanding*.

To Dee Reed for her editing help and advice.

To my many Muslim friends in the Republic of Chad.

To my wife, Sarah Gry, for her keen mind and inspirational heart.

Introduction

*Do not be afraid, for I am with you
I will bring your children from the east
And gather you from the west.*

Isaiah 43:5 (NIV)

On September 03, 2001, my identical twin brother, David, and I were returning from a long weekend in northern California. We had visited my aunt and uncle, and later gone to a wedding of one of David's ex-girlfriends. David and I usually end up fighting or arguing at some point if we spend more than a few hours together. This weekend, however, was different. We had a great time.

Before climbing the mountains that separate southern California from the central plain, we stopped to fill up on gas. An old sedan was sitting in the far corner of the lot with its hood open and a Hispanic family staring into it. David and I went over and greeted them in broken Spanish. It turned out to be a simple problem and the car was soon up and running. They waved goodbye as we got back in David's SUV to begin the last leg of our trip back to Glendale.

David's girlfriend was driving. David was in the passenger seat. My girlfriend and I were in the back. It was late, but coming at the end of a holiday weekend, traffic was heavy. I lay my head down in my girlfriend's lap and was soon asleep.

I awoke to the sudden, gut-wrenching feeling of a car lurching from side to side. I raised my head to look out between the two front seats just in time to see us swerving down the highway at about 70 mph right before rolling. As the car started to flip, time slowed down. I wasn't wearing my seatbelt, and as I headed toward the ceiling I heard a distinct voice telling me to relax, go with it, it'll be over soon and you'll be okay. Then I must have blacked out.

I awoke with my head face down toward my brother's feet. My body was lying on top of the emergency brake with my legs sticking up over the back seat. I looked up and saw David lying back in his reclined seat perfectly still as if he was asleep.

Immediately, someone was opening the back door behind us and saying we needed to get him out. I pulled myself up and my medical training automatically kicked in. I immobilized David's cervical spine with my two arms compressing his chest and back as one hand covered his chin and the other the back of his head.

Out of the corner of my eye I noticed a deformed mass at his right thigh through blood soaked jeans. In what seemed like a split second, David was out on the ground and I was doing chest compressions as an unknown woman gave rescue breaths. I glanced at David's head and noticed a large pool of dark blood forming on the asphalt.

I knew continuing CPR was hopeless. I stood up and walked over to the side of the road where the girls were shivering against the guardrail. Behind me, holiday traffic crawled by in one lane as our vehicle blocked the other three lanes. Miraculously, it was a single car accident.

After hours in the ER confirming I had nothing worse than broken ribs, a few cuts and a heavily bruised body that would feel much worse tomorrow, I wanted to call my parents but realized that I didn't have their new number. The only number that came to mind was my grandparents' in Florida. It was about 2:00 a.m. their time. Grandpa picked up.

"Hello?" came a groggy, raspy voice on the other end.

"Yeah, this is James. I need my parents' number."

"Whoa, what happened?"

"I'll explain later, can I just get the number?"

Grandpa quickly complied and I soon found myself talking to Mom on the other end.

"David's dead…"

As I heard my dad freak out and my mom calmly say they'd be on the first plane out it started to hit me: my identical twin brother and best (and maybe only) friend, was gone.

A whirlwind week of packing up David's apartment, receiving visitors and phone calls from all over the country, and preparing a memorial service first in California and then in Florida left me numb. The physical pain of the accident was coupled with a deep psychological ache that felt tangible.

Needless to say, two days after his burial on September 09, 2001, I was in no mood to comprehend the cataclysmic events that would change the world on 9-11. At that point, Muslims, Islam and Terrorism were confined to another universe that I'd briefly heard about, but never had an interest in. For me, the event that changed the world came and went without my giving Muslims another thought.

I finished my residency training in family medicine June 30, 2003, and a few months later found myself on a plane heading to the heart of Africa in the Republic of Chad. Suddenly, like it or not, I found myself surrounded by Muslims and Islamic culture. For several years, however, I still had no interest in learning about the religion proclaimed by almost 25% of the world's population. I was there to be a doctor after all, you know, save lives and stamp out disease and pestilence.

Little by little, however, I came to be fascinated and inspired by the people I'd kind of just grown up looking down on or ignoring at best. Islam began to intrigue me as I was exposed to it more and more in the people I was living and working with. I began to read books on Islam and even read through the Qur'an from cover to cover during the month of Ramadan in 2010. What I discovered over the course of those years in Chad was startling.

I was surprised to find out that many of the heroes of the Old Testament were either Arabs, tutored by Arabs or accompanied by Arabs on their missions. In fact, there is a whole other story weaving its thread through the pages of the ancient history of the Children of Israel: it is the story of the descendants of Ishmael, father of the Arabs. They are called the People or Children of the East.

Unlike what I'd been programmed to believe, Islam and the other great monotheistic faiths tracing their roots to Abraham actually had a long, documented history of working together up until a few hundred years ago. The history of the two sons of Abraham, Ishmael and Isaac and their offspring, known respectively as the Children of Israel and the Children of the East, was one of collaboration and cooperation.

Abraham gave all that he had to Isaac
But to the sons of Abraham's concubines, Abraham gave gifts
He sent them away from Isaac his son
While he yet lived, eastward, to the east country.

Genesis 25:5-6

When the West forgot about God and drifted into idolatry and apostasy, the East was there to bring them back and vice-versa. From Isaac and Ishmael to Joseph and the Ishmaelite traders; from Moses and Jethro to Balaam and Job; from Joshua and Caleb to Deborah and Jael; from Jehu and Jonadab to Jeremiah and the Rechabites; from the wise men at Jesus' birth to Paul and his years in Arabia; from the preservation of the Bible and containment of the Christian apostasy by Mohammed and the Arabs to the Protestant Reformation and the Ottoman Turks; the Children of Israel and the Children of the East have been working together to keep alive a knowledge of the true God, the Creator God, the God of Abraham, Isaac and Ishmael.

And what does that mean for us today and the War on Terrorism and the Middle East? It means it's up to us to reform and renew our covenant with God and collaborate as fellow believers like God originally intended. The story that follows is not a myth or a tall tale; it is the Biblical account of the spiritual heritage of Islam as told by the Children of the East.

Thus says Jehovah of Armies:
"Behold, I will save my people from the east country
And from the west country

Zechariah 8:7

Ishmael & Hagar

As for Ishmael, I have heard you
Behold, I have blessed him, and will make him fruitful
And will multiply him exceedingly
He will become the father of twelve princes
And I will make him a great nation.

Genesis 17:20

Praise be to God,
Who has given me Ishmael and Isaac
In spite of my age:
My Lord is indeed
One who hears prayer.

Qur'an 14:39

The red sun beats down mercilessly through the haze of the desert winds. Hagar can feel every bruise on her body as the adrenaline of her flight starts to wear off. The sand rubs the skin raw between her hennaed feet and her leather sandals as she shuffles slowly along. Her tears dry on her cheeks almost before they have time to trickle down her puffy face and blackened eyes.

Not sure exactly where she is, Hagar lifts her sagging head and looks around. Her flight has been sudden and blind. Thinking she recognizes a rock formation ahead, she picks up her pace until everything blends into the nothingness of this barren land.

If I remember correctly, there should be a well around here somewhere. And beyond, past the spring should be the road to Shur. But where am I going anyway? With this relentless heat pounding in my head, all I really want is a drink. Then, maybe I'll try and think this whole thing out.

Looking around Hagar knows there has to be a well close by. The signs are everywhere. Hoof marks and sandal prints have become more and more frequent as have the tiny piles of goat droppings and mounds of cattle and camel paddies. Just ahead, beside an acacia tree, she sees some twisted logs placed together around what appears to be a hole. The smooth wood marked with grooves along the edges betrays the presence of water. Years of heavy, dripping bags made of camel stomachs tied to hand woven ropes dragged over the edges of the lumber have formed the deep notches.

As she lets the pouch down into the abyss, she wonders if she'll have the strength to haul it back up again. Finally slaking her thirst Hagar leans back against the acacia tree hoping to catch a little rest in its meager shade.

The hot wind continues to blow across her face. Hagar pulls her veil up close to keep the dust out of her mouth and nose. Closing her eyes against the hot wind, she tries to recall the events that have led up to today.

It was during the time of the famine that Hagar first started traveling with Abram and Sarai. The rich couple had come to Egypt to find food. Despite their wealth, they didn't have many servants to protect them. Abram was afraid that Pharaoh would kill him to take his beautiful wife. So he lied and said Sarai was his sister. All of Pharaoh's friends and advisors told him how beautiful Sarai was. After giving Abram many gifts of sheep, oxen, donkeys and slaves, Pharaoh took Sarai into his harem. As one of the harem staff, Hagar was assigned to be Sarai's personal assistant.

Abram didn't know what to do except pray to his God. Sarai was saved when Pharaoh and his household all became sick with the plague. The Egyptian king soon recognized that it must be the powerful God of Abram behind it all. After questioning the patriarch and learning the truth, he gave Sarai back. Thankfully, he hadn't yet slept with her. Pharaoh then sent them on their way with all the gifts he'd already given Abram, with the addition of Hagar who continued as Sarai's handmaid.

During her close interaction with Sarai and Abram, Hagar grew to admire them greatly. She saw their faithfulness to God. She witnessed Abram, the chief of the clan, bow to the wishes of his nephew, Lot, and let him choose the richer pastures of the plains near Sodom and Gomorrah, humbly giving up his rights for the sake of peace.

Later, when Lot was captured and then rescued by Abram, Hagar observed Abram's dedication in giving a tenth of all the plunder to Melchizedek, the King of Salem and high priest of God Most High. Abram then returned the other 90% to those he had rescued, refusing to profit from someone else's misfortune. Hagar couldn't help but be impressed and in her heart started praying to the God of Abram.

Of course, Hagar knew of the promises God had made to Abram to make him a great nation. She also knew of Abram and Sarai's frustration at their infertility. They'd been married a long time, yet had no children. But, Abram still believed that despite his and Sarai's advanced ages (Abram was 85 years old and Sarai was 75), God would somehow accomplish his plan for their life and give them an heir.

Hagar had no clue that would involve her until that fateful day less than a year ago. Without warning, Sarai called her into her tent one evening and explained that Hagar was now going to be Abram's concubine so that they could have a child through her. No one had asked her opinion. Of course, she'd thought she'd get married someday. She'd entered puberty several years ago and had started to enjoy that fact that some of the young servant boys noticed her developing womanhood. She imagined she'd probably fall in love with one of them some day and of course have children.

But the thought had never entered Hagar's head that the father of her children would be old enough to be her great grandfather. Of course, she didn't have a choice. She was just a common slave girl after all. Who was she to resist the local customs? Many rich men took young wives and concubines from among their servants, especially if the first wife was barren. Then, the children of the concubine were raised by the wife and considered her own. Her life was forever changed.

Hagar tried to stay positive. At least, Abram was a Godly man. He treated her gently and kindly. He was kind of uncomfortable with the idea himself, but felt he had to listen to his wife's advice. Two months after going in to Abram, Hagar was already pregnant. She couldn't help but feel proud despite the fatigue and nausea of the first three months. Then, when she felt the baby start to move inside her she couldn't help but be excited. She didn't mean to rub it in to Sarai that she had gotten pregnant while Sarai had tried for decades without success. But when she went in to let Sarai feel the baby's kick, she was shocked when Sarai got up quickly and stalked out the door of the tent.

Wasn't this what Sarai wanted? Hagar was confused. Suddenly, things changed. Sarai yelled at her all the time and for the slightest thing would slap her or even beat her. Finally, one day, when Hagar was really starting to show her pregnancy, Sarai went too far. Hagar spilled some camel's milk all over Sarai's favorite prayer rug and her mistress became furious. But Hagar was young and strong and instead of taking the beating like a good slave, she fled.

So now here she is, in the desert. Hagar opens her gritty eyes and licks her parched lips.

What's that over by the well? It looks like a man coming toward me. Have I been followed and found already? Is this one of Abram's servants coming to drag me back and give me the punishment I deserve: death as a runaway slave? Or is it one of the ruthless local shepherds? If so, what can I do? Most likely I'll be raped, beaten and left for dead.

The man approaches slowly, giving Hagar time to take him in. Of average height, his unkempt hair flows out from under his loosely wound turban. A scraggly beard surrounds a face wrinkled and tanned, probably from years of harsh desert life. As the man strides easily toward her in his simple robes, Hagar notices the kindness in his deep, brown eyes. Stopping at a respectful distance, he greets her in a soft, confident voice.

"Peace be upon you." The stranger says as he raises his right hand and then moves it toward his heart, lightly touching his chest as his head bows slightly.

"And peace be upon you, sir." Hagar replies.

"Hagar, Sarai's maid, where have you come from?" the man asks. "And where are you going?"

How does he know me? As she looks intently into the man's rugged, ageless face she's confident she's never seen him before. Somehow, though, he seems familiar and his presence comforts her troubled spirit. She decides to be honest.

"I'm running away from my mistress."

"Return to Sarai and submit to her." As the man continues to speak, the slow realization comes upon her: this is no mere man; this is the God of Abram himself. "I will make you into a great nation. Yes, you are pregnant and you will have a son and you will call him Ishmael because God has heard your prayers."

Hagar bows respectfully to the ground, her forehead touching the hot sand, her hands spread out in prostration before God. Ishmael…God hears. Hagar begins to weep softly. *God has indeed heard my cries!*

"This son of yours will be a wild and free man. He will be against everyone and everyone will be against him. He will live near his relatives, but in the eastern lands."

Just as suddenly as he'd appeared, he disappears. However, Hagar senses that in some strange way, he is still present. *Lahai Roi. He is the Living One Who Sees Me!* Feeling peace in her heart, and a renewed strength in her body she feels she can trust that God will keep his promise. *I should follow his advice. I should go back. I will submit as much as possible, no matter how painful it may be.*

Hagar returns to the camp and meekly takes up her post, serving Sarai in complete submission to her will. However she can't keep silent about her encounter with God. The story spreads around the region and people begin to call that special place, *Bir Lahai Roi.*

A few months later, Ishmael is born, screaming and kicking.

As the baby grows, Hagar and Sarai form a fragile truce. After Ishmael is weaned, he's always with Abram or Sarai, so Hagar rarely sees him. They want to make sure everyone knows whose child he is considered to be. Ishmael spends hours sitting on Abram's lap and hearing the tales of his ancestors. He loves the story about Adam and Eve and the serpent. Cringing when Cain kills his brother Abel, Ishmael rejoices when Enoch is taken directly to heaven. Whenever it rains, Abram reminds him of the flood and whenever they see a rainbow, Ishmael's father tells him of God's promise to never again destroy the world with water. When Abram tells him of the Tower of Babel and the wickedness of men, the young boy cries in sorrow.

But Ishmael's favorite stories of all are his father's own stories: how he left his hometown Ur with Grandpa Terah only to bury him later in Haran. He listens delightedly to the tales of traveling to Egypt during the famine, rescuing Uncle Lot, giving the tithe to Melchizedek, and Ishmael's own birth predicted by the Angel of God at *Bir Lahai Roi.*

Abram constantly reminds Ishmael that God has a special purpose for his life. God has never before made promises about someone having descendants like the stars of the sky or the sand of the shore. Since Adam and Eve, God has never appeared to people in human form and he's never named someone before they were born. Even Abram himself only heard God speak through visions. But with Ishmael, God appeared directly to his mom. So, Abram reminds Ishmael constantly that if God chose to do things he had never done before, it was because Ishmael is unusually important. God definitely has a plan for him and his descendants.

When Ishmael becomes a teenager, God appears to Abram again in a vision and renews His promises. God changes Abram's name to Abraham and Sarai's to Sarah. He also tells Abraham that as a sign of their agreement, all the men in the household have to be circumcised. So, when Abraham is 99 years old and Ishmael is 13, they both have their foreskins cut off on the same day. Thus, Ishmael officially becomes a part of the covenant between God and Abraham.

A few months later, God finally appears in human form to Abraham. Ishmael is sitting with Abraham under the big tree at Mamre when three men walk up the hill. Being a noble host, Abraham orders a feast prepared and they all eat together. Afterwards, Ishmael listens in wide-eyed disbelief as Abraham dares to debate with the leader of the group over the fate of

Sodom and Gomorrah. As the conversation progresses, Ishmael realizes that this is the same God in human form who appeared to Hagar in the desert. He is amazed as he hears his father argue with God. What a surprise to learn that God likes having friends who are not afraid, but who want to reason with him and understand his purposes.

After the destruction of Sodom and Gomorrah, Abraham and Ishmael move south to the Negev and go to the city of Gerar where Abraham again lies about Sarah, saying she is his sister. Ishmael witnesses again how God intervenes to save his father's wife's honor despite Abraham's dishonorable act.

About this time, Sarah finds out she's pregnant. Ishmael is excited to know he'll finally have a sibling. It's incredible to him that as old as Abraham and Sarah are, that she could get pregnant. Obviously it is only the God he's getting to know that could have accomplished such a miracle. After nine months, Sarah gives birth to Ishmael's half-brother Isaac, who is circumcised eight days later, as a sign that just like Ishmael, he is a part of the covenant given to Abraham.

Things go well as Ishmael grows into his mid-teens and continues to be mentored by Abraham. But then, one careless act on his part and everything changes for Ishmael and Hagar.

The day starts out well with a big celebration. It is Isaac's second birthday and it's time for him to be weaned. During the feast, as older brothers are prone to do, Ishmael begins imitating some of Isaac's silly faces and gestures. Everyone else laughs good-naturedly, but Sarah's face turns to stone. Later that evening, after everyone else has gone to bed, she enters Abraham's tent.

"Get rid of that slave girl and her son." Sarah demands, "My son Isaac isn't going to share his inheritance with anyone!"

Shocked, Abraham doesn't know what to say. Sarah storms out, leaving Abraham alone with his troubled thoughts. As is his habit, he lifts his hands and his eyes to heaven and seeks counsel from God. God doesn't let him down as the still small voice speaks again to Abraham's heart.

"Don't be upset over Ishmael or Hagar. Do as Sarah says, for it's through Isaac that I'll fulfill my covenant. Just as I promised before, though, I'll also make Ishmael into a great nation, because he is also your son."

A few days and a blur of preparations later, Hagar finds herself again in the desert. It is all too familiar: same sand, same wind, same dust, same sun, same heat, and same thirst. This time, instead of fleeing, it is Abraham himself who has sent her away. She wanders aimlessly in the direction of *Bir Sheba* in southern Arabia. This time, however, she is a little better prepared. Abraham has given her food and a goatskin of water. Besides, this time she isn't alone. Her 15-year-old son Ishmael is with her.

Finally, though, the water is gone and Ishmael starts to die of thirst. Out in the desert, oases are few and far between, and if one doesn't know the desert well, one can wander in circles for days and weeks without finding water. Hagar and Ishmael don't even have camels to give them a chance. There's no more hope. Ishmael's lips are cracked and bleeding. His face is peeling from the wind and sun. His eyes are swollen shut and his breathing is shallow as he sinks into a sand dune.

Hagar gathers what little strength she has and drags him under the shade of a thorn bush. Then she crawls about 100 feet away, lays prostrate in the sand and begins to sob wildly, her tears evaporating quickly in the relentless sand. With her final ounce of force, she lifts her head and cries out to God.

"I don't want to watch him die!"

God hears. Some rough hands shake Hagar awake and pull her to her knees. She looks up into the same eternal face she saw once, 15 years before. The same voice comforts her again in her affliction.

"Hagar, what's wrong? Don't be afraid!" The voice is compassionate and heavy with emotion. "God has heard the boy's cries. Go and comfort him, for I will make of him a great nation."

Hagar stumbles over to where Ishmael lays and as she does, lifts her eyes to the horizon. *Is it a mirage? How could she have missed it?* Ishmael revives enough to follow his mom as they shuffle over on unsteady feet to a crystal clear spring of water gushing out of the sands a few feet away. They fall face down in the water. After drinking their fill, they lift up their faces and hands to the sky, praising the God of Abraham, Isaac and Ishmael. God has heard their cries!

The Bible says in Genesis 21:20-21 that "God was with the boy as he grew up. He lived in the desert and became an archer. While he was living in the Desert of Paran, his mother got a wife for him from Egypt."

According to Islamic tradition, Abraham visited Ishmael three times in the desert. During the last visit, they together built an altar to the Creator God. The structure later came to be known as the Ka'ba, the object of the various pilgrimages to Makkah down through the centuries.

Meanwhile, Isaac grew up and Sarah died. Isaac married his cousin, Rebekah. Abraham took Keturah as a wife and had six sons by her: Zimran, Jokshan, Medan, Midian, Ishbak, and Shuah. Jokshan's two sons were named Sheba and Dedan.

Isaac inherited most of Abraham's wealth, but all his other sons, including Ishmael, got a portion. However, Abraham sent them off into the East, away from Isaac, where most of them became desert nomads and traders: the ancestors of the Arabs. Isaac had only two sons, Jacob and Esau.

One evening, God gave Jacob a different, special name. From then on, he was called Israel. So, the descendants of Abraham from Isaac came to be known as the Israelites, or the Children of Israel. The other descendants of Abraham intermarried and came to be known as the Ishmaelites, the Midianites or the Children of the East.

Like many brothers the world over, Isaac and Ishmael have had their ups and downs. But God had a special plan for these two: cooperation. To symbolize this, despite their estrangement, when Abraham died, Isaac and Ishmael were reunited. Isaac came from the West, Ishmael from the East and together they buried their father. Together they wept and remembered the promises of God who changed their father's name from Abram (Exalted Father) to Abraham (Father of Many Nations).

And as they parted ways again, little did they know that God's plan was for these two mighty nations to continue to work together throughout the rest of human history all the way until the end of time. First though, came the story of Isaac's grandson, Joseph and his amazing rescue by the Ishmaelites...

Joseph & the Ishmaelites

Joseph said to them
"Don't be afraid, for am I in the place of God?
As for you, you meant evil against me
But God meant it for good, to bring to pass
As it is this day, to save many people alive.

Genesis 50:19-20

Then there came a caravan of travelers
They sent their water-carrier,
And he let down his bucket into the well
He said: "Ah there! Good news!
Here is a fine young man!"
So they concealed him as a treasure!

Qur'an 12:19

Joseph's head bobs back and forth in rhythm with the swaying of the camel's back. His throat is parched, his belly empty, his rear sore from lack of riding experience and his body bruised from the fall. Even though his new owners had quickly removed the ropes tearing into his wrists he knows he is not free. *In these burning sands, even if I managed to get down from the camel without killing myself, there's nowhere to go. Only a seasoned Bedouin could hope to find his way amongst these endless, identical mountains of sand...we must be in the Negev by now.*

As he drifts in and out of an exhausted sleep, Joseph's mind wanders back to the events that have led up to this drastic change in his life circumstances. It's hard to believe that just a few days ago...*how many was it now?*...he was the privileged favorite son of a wealthy nomadic chieftain with a bright future in front of him.

It all started with his dreams…

"*Abba, Abba*, listen to this, it's crazy!" Joseph was bursting with excitement as he rushed into his father's tent. "You won't believe it, I had another dream just as bizarre as the first one."

"Okay, okay, calm down, Joseph," Jacob patted the mat to his right, gesturing for Joseph to sit beside him. "Well then, what is it this time?"

"Remember last time when I dreamed I was out with my brothers harvesting the grain and then all their bundles of hay bowed down to mine? Well, this time it was the sun, moon and stars. And I don't know how to explain, but you know how weird dreams can be…they all bowed down to me in a sign of deep respect. What do you think it all means?"

Jacob sat quietly for a while and Joseph could tell he was troubled. In fact, it seemed like he was fighting to control his anger. Joseph's eyes widened and his heart sank. This was not the reaction he expected.

Finally, Jacob spoke in guarded, tightly controlled tones. "Who…do you…think….you…are? Do you think that now not only your brothers but my wives and I are going to bow down to you as well? Be your servants or something? Get out of here, and if I was you, I'd forget all this dreaming and learn to do something practical for a change!"

Joseph backed out quickly from the tent and ran off into the bush, tears drying on his cheeks almost as fast as they fell. He didn't understand. It wasn't his fault he had the dream, or was it? He was confused as he fell to his knees and prayed to his God, the God of Abraham, Isaac and Ishmael. Peace filled his soul and after a few hours he quietly returned to camp.

No matter what he did, it seemed he irritated his brothers. All older than him, they were a motley crew. Rough and cruel, they'd learned to survive on the edge of the desert. Joseph and his sensitivity to spiritual things were a constant source of jokes to the older brothers. It didn't help that they all knew that Joseph's mom was the favorite wife of Jacob.

The final straw was when, during one of the lean years, only Joseph got new clothes and what fine ones they were! Meanwhile, the other 11 brothers and their sister, Dinah, had to make do with last year's ragged leftovers.

One day, they all vowed, they'd get their revenge.

That day came all too soon. Reuben, Simeon, Judah and the others were all out with the sheep searching for better grazing. They'd been gone for a week and Jacob was starting to worry. He had an idea where they'd be, so he sent out Joseph to look for them.

Joseph put on his new robe and wrapped his turban tight around his head and throat. With his smoothly polished cattle stick in one hand and a goatskin with cheese, butter, bread and dates in the other, he took off barefoot through the bush. Avoiding the prickly thorn bushes, the young teenager followed the trail left by hundreds of sheep and cattle droppings.

After several days wandering and barely missing his father's herds, Joseph finally spotted them from the top of a low hill. They were down in a wadi, nibbling what grass was left from last year's rains. He could see what looked like his brothers scattered among the flocks and resting in the shade of the ubiquitous acacia trees.

Joseph scrambled down the boulders, eagerly anticipating being reunited with his brothers and bringing them the news from camp. He never knew what hit him. A movement out of the corner of his eye and a large staff swinging rapidly toward his face was the last thing he remembered.

What must have been several hours later, Joseph woke up to find himself in the bottom of a dry well at least 100 feet deep. He felt blood still wet and sticky on his face and his whole body ached, probably from the fall. He carefully checked his wrists, arms, hands, legs and feet but didn't seem to have any obvious broken bones. He wearily pulled himself to his feet and looked up.

The opening was covered with logs except in the middle where the water bags made of camel stomachs were lowered hand over hand to fetch the life-giving water that was no longer there. The well seemed to have been abandoned years ago. Off in a corner, the whitened bones of some unknown animal reflected the dim sunlight from above. The walls were sheer and slick, a mixture of rock and clay and impossible to climb. Joseph was stuck.

Occasionally he heard voices muttering nearby, often raised in argument. He got the impression that more than once, a fight almost broke out. His thoughts were in a whirl. *What happened? Did bandits attack me? There are a lot in this area, but it would be unlikely to be attacked and left like this without attracting the attention of my brothers. What's going on?*

Slowly, but determinedly the thought entered his head unwanted. *Maybe it was...my brothers.* The more Joseph thought about it, the more he came to believe what he would've never thought possible. His own family had attacked him, beat him up, thrown him in a pit and left him for dead.

Joseph's thoughts drifted back to the stories of Abraham he'd heard all his life, God's covenant, the destruction of Sodom and Gomorrah, and Abraham bargaining with God over roast veal. He remembered how his own father had fled from Grandfather Isaac and Uncle Esau after deceiving them. He thought of Jacob's dream of a ladder to heaven and how he had wrestled with the angel all night before being touched by God himself.

God has always been so real in the life of my ancestors...is he there for me as well?

It shocked him to think that his brothers, who had also grown up hearing those same stories, could treat him as worse than a slave. *What are they up to now? Is it all a cruel joke or just another dream? Or are they really planning to kill me?*

Joseph was jolted out of his reverie by a shadow blocking the sunlight from the well opening. A rough camelhair rope bounced down in front of him almost hitting him in the face.

"Hey, ya little punk, grab hold, okay?" A gruff voice he recognized as his brother Judah's growled from above.

Joseph had no choice. He slowly worked his way hand over hand, pushing off the slick walls of the well with his calloused feet as best he could. Finally, near the top, several heavily muscled, hairy arms reached down to pull him the rest of the way out.

The sunlight hurt his eyes at first and Joseph heard the camels before he saw them. Dirty and treacherous, they seemed to be eyeing him to see which one would get the privilege of making his life miserable. Simeon and Levi held Joseph tight, their dirty fingernails biting into his arms. Near the head of the caravan, Judah and the rest of the boys were in deep discussion with the turbaned nomads.

Joseph had heard stories of these wandering desert wolves. When grandfather Isaac's older brother Ishmael had been driven into the desert with his mother Hagar, he had learned quickly how to not only survive, but to thrive in that harsh environment. Using his skill as an archer, Ishmael soon developed a reputation as a man to be feared and respected. With his fierce dedication to the God of his father, Abraham, Ishmael soon became a leader among the desert peoples.

Ishmael had 12 sons and a couple of daughters. Keeping things in the family, the Ishmaelites soon came to dominate the trade routes bringing frankincense and myrrh from the southern Arabian Peninsula. After awhile, Abraham's other sons, born in his old age to his third wife, Ketourah, joined the descendants of Ishmael in the desolate sands. In fact, the Midianites, descended from Abraham's son, Midian, worked so closely with the Ishmaelites that they were thought of as one and the same people. Even Uncle Esau intermarried by taking Ishmael's daughter, Basemath, as his wife. Because of where they all lived in relation to Isaac and Jacob's direct relatives, they also were known collectively as the Children of the East.

The bargaining carried on for what seemed like hours before Joseph saw money change hands and the leader of the caravan started walking over to where Joseph sat cross-legged in the sand, his hands tied roughly behind his back.

The man was of average height and wore a simple robe gathered at his waist by a camel hair belt. His legs were bare, powerful and darkened by years under the desert sun. His face was covered by the ends of his turban to keep out the dust and protect his mouth and nose from the blasts of hot winds whipping across the dunes. Only his dark eyes showed: sharp and shrewd, but not unkind.

"Peace be upon you, brother." The nomad chieftain squatted in front of Joseph. "I am Sheba, son of Jokshan, grandson of Abraham. You will be coming with us to Egypt."

Simeon pulled Joseph roughly to his feet and shoved him in the direction of the retreating Bedouin. "Off you go, ya little brat. See how you like the desert for a bit. No more cushy special favors for our spoiled little brother, eh?" With that the other brothers laughed and turned away as Joseph stumbled toward the waiting camels...

"Joseph! Joseph! Hey, boy, wake up!" The cry jolts Joseph back to the present and the painful reality of his camel. He sees Sheba watching him, a concerned look in his eyes. "You'll fall of the camel and break your neck if you keep falling asleep like that. Focus, one step at a time, that's the way to survive in the desert. Don't give up ever, don't think too far ahead, make the best of any situation, always be generous, never eat alone and remember, in the end, it's all in God's hands anyway. Follow that advice and you just might make it."

Joseph wonders again at the faith of these distant relatives of his. He had become accustomed to thinking of all others outside of his own immediate family as pagans and idolaters. Pretty much wherever Jacob moved his tents, they were surrounded by people worshipping idols, nature, the sun, moon, stars and pretty much anything else one could think of. His family's insistence that there was only one God that was invisible and all-powerful met with general mockery among their neighbors.

But in the weeks that he's spent with the Ishmaelites, Joseph has come to respect not only their toughness mixed with kindness, but their dedication to God. Morning and evening and throughout the day they pause to pray, their faces toward the East and their hands upturned to receive God's blessings. At night around the fires, they tell the same stories he heard as a child of the creation of the world, Adam and Eve, the Garden of Eden and the serpent, Noah and the flood, the tower of Babel, the division of the earth in the time of Peleg and Joktan, and, of course, the tales of Abraham, Isaac and Ishmael and the covenant God made with each one.

Joseph starts to spend more and more time in prayer as well. With each jolt of his aching body, he feels he can't handle a step further. But each time, he feels some new energy being poured into his body as he senses the presence of Something else around him as he never has before.

One morning, after just a few miles of marching, a cry goes up from the lead camel. "The pyramids! The pyramids! Egypt at last!" After days of nothing but sand, sun and heat, Joseph finds himself looking at palm trees, houses and a bustling market filled with meat and fruits he couldn't have imagined, even in his wildest dreams.

Sheba brings the caravan to a halt. As the others began unloading their merchandise, Sheba takes Joseph through some narrow side alleys. After a few minutes, they arrive at the edge of a narrow, open courtyard with people milling about in expectation.

Sheba grabs Joseph by both shoulders and looks him intensely in the eyes. "I hate to do this. You're my brother after all, and I've grown quite fond of you. But business is business. I somehow get the feeling that what I'm about to do is the right thing even though it may not seem that way to you at first. I've prayed a lot about it…and well, you have to trust in God, no matter what happens.

"I'll try and make sure you get into good hands. The bottom line is: I can't afford another mouth to feed, and I have to get back the money I invested in you or we'll all starve. I didn't really want to buy you from those shifty brothers of yours, but I had a feeling you'd be better off out of their hands.

"So, listen to me: don't cry whatever you do. Be a man and remember the advice I gave you on the camel that day. One day at a time and leave it in God's hands. Follow me."

With that, Sheba turns and brings Joseph into a tiny room off to the side of the square. After speaking in whispers to a short, bearded man in the corner, Sheba returns to Joseph's side.

"I've spoken to my brother, also one of us, and he'll make sure you get sold into good hands. He says that a respected man in the government, Potiphar, captain of the king's guards, is looking for some house help. That'll keep you out of the labor camps where they literally work you to death making bricks, cutting stone, hauling water and harvesting grain."

Sheba looks Joseph intently in the eyes. "Okay, you're in good hands." Kissing Joseph on both cheeks, he turns to go. "May God's peace rest on you!" With that, he's gone.

So Joseph is sold into slavery in Egypt. Through faithfulness and honesty he is soon made the head of Potiphar's household until one day, Potiphar's wife tries to seduce him. Joseph runs and Potiphar's wife accuses him of attempted rape, landing him in prison. By interpreting the dreams of two other inmates, his case finally comes before Pharaoh, king of Egypt, when he himself has a dream that needs interpreting. Joseph interprets the dream and gives such good advice on how to deal with the foreseen famine that Pharaoh makes him Prime Minister. Using wisely the power of his new post, Joseph is able to save not only Egypt, but his own family who comes to buy grain during the famine. Joseph is reunited with his family who he brings to Egypt. His forgiveness of his brothers is legendary.

Sheba and his fellow traders continued to travel the deserts of the Middle East telling the story of how they rescued the new vizier of Egypt from certain death. One night, around a campfire in the town of Pethor, a young orphan named Balaam hears the tale and it changes his life.

Unfortunately after Pharaoh's death, the new ruler of Egypt enslaves the children of Israel for 400 years. Degraded by the drudgery of their lives, the descendants of Isaac all but forget the God of Abraham. Meanwhile, in the desert, the worship of the true God flourishes, especially in the deserts of Midian where the priest, Jethro Reuel, lives with his seven daughters and their flocks of sheep.

Back in Egypt, despite the decree of Pharaoh to kill all newborn Israelite boys, one mother saves her son by hiding him in a basket made of reeds that she sets afloat down the Nile. As the new Pharaoh's daughter bathes one day, she sees the basket and rescues the child. She takes the boy into the palace to raise him as her own giving him the name Moses...

Jethro & Moses

Jethro rejoiced for all the goodness
Which Jehovah had done...
"Blessed be Jehovah, who has delivered you
Out of the hand of the Egyptians...
Now I know that Jehovah is greater than all gods"

Exodus 18:9-11

Then you killed someone,
but We rescued you from distress,
And We subjected you to trials.
Then you sojourned for years among the Midianites.
Now you have come, O Moses, according to destiny.
And I have selected you for My own purpose.
Go, you and your brother, with My signs.
Let neither of you tire of remembering Me...
Do not fear, for I am with you;
I hear and I see.

Qur'an 20:40-42, 46

How much time has passed? Moses wonders as he stumbles through
the desolate valleys. The towering dunes seem to stretch on forever on both
sides. *How long have I been trudging along?* His weary mind and
dehydrated body refuse to cooperate. The only thing certain in his life right
now is the blistering heat of the day and the chilling cool of the desert
night. *At least I have enough water.*

Weeks before, Moses' military training had kicked in automatically as
he rapidly prepared to flee. Body on autopilot, he had slung several water
skins over his shoulders, stuffed a knife into his belt, hung a slingshot over

the knife handle, wrapped a turban around his head, strapped on his least-worn sandals and slipped furtively through all the secret passages in Pharaoh's palace till he reached the Nile.

As he crouched in the rushes along the banks of the broad river his mind was drawn irresistibly back to the stories his adoptive mother told him of how he came to be a prince of Egypt.

Moses, Moses. I drew you out of the water. That's what your name means, my child. The gods gave you to me ten years ago. I felt I had been cursed. I couldn't have children. But one day, as I went as usual to the Mother of all Rivers to bathe, there you were. The most perfect boy of them all floating down to me on the bosom of the Nile in a little basket: a gift from the gods.

You were nursed by a Hebrew but raised to be a King. You have a divine destiny, my son, to lead and rule. Do it with fairness and justice, but don't be afraid to do whatever it takes to become what you were meant to be.

Moses never forgot those words. They were a constant source of inspiration as he progressed rapidly through the best educational system of the world's most powerful empire. He was schooled in the arts, the sciences, magic, religion, war, government, law, hieroglyphics, and diplomacy. He was taller, stronger, smarter, faster and more stubborn than the other royal boys in Pharaoh's large household and soon became their ringleader.

For 40 years, he received the best that the world's superpower had to offer and his future was bright. It was almost guaranteed that when the current Pharaoh died, the Council would name Moses to replace him.

But Moses had a secret that only his Egyptian mother knew. At least, she was the only Egyptian who knew. Moses was the son of a slave. But he kept that secret buried deep. He never let his guard down. Nothing would stop him from becoming King.

However, Moses did have a weakness: his temper. He used it often to his advantage to intimidate and manipulate his opponents. But sometimes it betrayed him as it caused him to lose his carefully cultivated control.

Coming back to the present, Moses shakes off his reverie and pulls himself to his feet. *Got to keep moving.* He takes a swig of water to refresh his parched throat and continues his slow progress through the rocky wilderness of the Sinai Peninsula. *I ought to be close to the border of Midian or somewhere in northern Arabia.*

Trudging on, Moses stops up short. *There it is again. No...can it be? Impossible! Am I losing my mind?* Everywhere Moses looks, he sees the man's face: outlined in the side of an embankment, staring at him from a dark crevice, looking up at him from the pale sand. It is the face of the first man he ever killed.

It had all started off so innocently. One day, he decided to visit the Hebrew camp. Never had he seen such poverty. Being isolated on the royal palace grounds, he was unaware of the living conditions of the Hebrew slaves. Mud huts with thatched roofs piled on top of each other as naked children ran through the mud, sewage and trash that filled the narrow alleyways. Blank stares looked up from meager rations as the women desperately tried to get enough strength back in their men so they wouldn't collapse on the job as the slowly raised the titanic projects of Pharaoh.

Moses wandered out to the work site. Hundreds of slaves moved as robots in and out of the massive piles of stones slowly taking the shape of an image of the Great Pharaoh. Around a corner, hidden in the shade of an obelisk, Moses came upon an Egyptian beating a slave. Something inside of Moses snapped. His vision grew dark, his mind closed to all reason and his muscles tensed.

Moses sprang on the Egyptian like a cat on a mouse. His years of military training and superb physical conditioning made quick work of the taskmaster. In a few seconds the man lay lifeless at his feet, his neck twisted at an odd angle. Moses looked at the slave who stared wide-eyed in shock before quickly backing up and then fleeing around the corner. Thinking quickly, Moses grabbed a shovel and quickly buried the corpse in the sand.

It hadn't taken long for the rumors to get around that an important overseer had been found murdered and that someone was claiming to be a witness. Despite his regrets and the return of his reason, Moses knew he could never undo that one passionate act. So, he fled.

And now, here I am, in the desert, far from everything I once knew and enjoyed. His water running low, Moses knows he can't last much longer. He has to find a well and some food to eat. Just then, looking up ahead he sees a welcome site: a few goats standing silhouetted against the midday sun on the top of the dune. There must be an oasis nearby.

Sure enough, a few hundred yards later, Moses rounds a corner and comes upon a well-used spring. He pulls himself up some water and then sits on the edge to rest. Soon, a huge flock of sheep and goats comes up herded by seven young girls who look enough alike they're probably sisters. Barefoot, with simple robes down to their ankles, scarves draped haphazardly over wild black hair and flowers woven in and out of their long tresses, they are the picture of innocence and beauty.

Giggling and skipping, they come to the well and start drawing water to put in the troughs for the animals. They glance shyly from time to time at the weirdly dressed stranger, but for the most part ignore the ragged young man.

Suddenly, around the corner marches another troop of cattle and donkeys pushed along by the shouts of some rough looking young men. Four of them sidle up and shove the girls out of the way.

"Thanks for getting some water for our herds. Now, back off ya pretty young things if you know what's good for you!" snarls one of the shepherds as he glares menacingly at the girls.

Quickly backing up, the seven young ladies sit sullenly on some rocks in the shade of a towering cliff to the south. They toss pebbles into the sand and mutter amongst themselves, but seem resigned to their daily fate.

Moses feels a burning anger start to course through his veins. He's always had a strong sense of justice and fair play. Hating to see the strong prey on the weak, he's always rooted for the underdog—unless the underdog was his own opponent. Slowly rising to his feet, Moses catches the unruly men's attention.

"Peace be unto you, stranger." The ringleader speaks warily. "Where you come from with them fancy clothes of yours?"

"It's not your affair," replies Moses, his voice even. "Why don't you just let the girls water their flocks first? They did get here before you, you know."

"Well, isn't that something! This stranger wants us to let the girls go first. Well, let me tell you something, boy, I don't take orders from nobody round here, got it? So, if you want some trouble, stick around because you just found it…"

Almost before the man can finish his sentence, Moses springs on him, twists him to the ground and puts his knife to his throat.

"I was wondering if you wouldn't like to reconsider your position, my friend. Why not let the girls water their flocks right now instead of waiting for you dirty old men, how does that sound? And if you'd like to leave here as a living breathing scumbag instead of a dead one, why don't you tell your friends over there to make a quick about face and take your mangy cattle elsewhere for a few hours until these girls finish?"

As the others slowly back away, Moses ties up the suddenly meek bully. Handing the knife to the oldest girl so she can stand guard, Moses draws from the well to water the herds. When all the animals have drunk their fill, the girls run back gleefully to tell their father the story.

Moses cuts the poor captive shepherd loose and slowly follows after the girls. Soon the oldest comes running back and breathlessly invites him to come for dinner in her father's tent. As Moses approaches the tent, a dignified man with gray hair peeking out from under his head covering opens the flap and greets him in the way of the Children of the East.

"May peace be upon you, stranger." The man extends his hand in greeting. "My name is Reuel, priest of Midian and father of the girls you rescued today. Come, eat with me."

Sitting down to a sumptuous feast of roasted lamb, curds and dates, Moses feels at home immediately. He finds out that as a descendant of Abraham's son Midian, Reuel is called Jethro (His Excellence) because of his position in the clan as high priest of the God of Abraham.

Reuel tells an amazed Moses the stories of the Creation, Adam and Eve, Noah and the flood, Abraham, Isaac and Ishmael. It is Reuel that has kept alive the promises made to Abraham, ensuring that the worship of God remains unstained by the many idols of the surrounding tribes. He has spent years in the desert praying and communing with God. He heard of the suffering of his distant cousins from the tribe of Israel, and is happy to welcome one of them into his home.

Moses quickly settles into the nomadic, herder lifestyle of his adopted family. Not having heard much about the true God since leaving his nursemaid for the courts of Pharaoh, he drinks up the stories of God that Reuel tells around the fires at night. He soon falls in love with Reuel's oldest daughter, Zipporah, and the two are married. Moses spends most of his days wandering the desert with Reuel's herds, protecting them from danger and making sure they have enough to eat.

Despite the harsh lifestyle, especially compared to the comforts of Egypt, Moses welcomes the chance to be alone with God. He learns to hear God's still, small voice speak to him in the silences of the desert and the mountains. Whenever he has questions about what God is like, he finds ready answers in the wise counsel of his father-in-law.

Forty years come and go under the tutelage of the priest of Midian. Finally, God decides that Moses is ready to finally fulfill the destiny for which he has been preparing him during the last 80 years. So, God speaks to Moses from a burning bush on Mount Sinai and tells him to go back to Egypt and free his brothers from slavery. It is here that God tells Moses his name: *Jehovah.* This name is so holy that ever after the Hebrews refuse to pronounce it. Instead, when they read God's name out loud, they say *Adonai.*

Moses obeys and returns to Egypt. On the way, Jehovah sends an angel to kill Moses. Despite what Reuel has been teaching him about the covenant with Abraham and the symbol of circumcision, Moses didn't circumcise his sons, Gershom and Eliezer. Thinking quickly, Zipporah takes a flint knife and cuts off both boys' foreskins, thus saving Moses' life. Moses realizes that he still hasn't completely surrendered to Jehovah, but decides to take Jehovah and his calling more seriously. Understanding the importance and danger of his mission, Moses sends Zipporah, Gershom and Eliezer back to Reuel while he continues on to Egypt.

In Egypt, Moses meets with resistance from Pharaoh until all ten of the infamous plagues are accomplished, including the death of all the first-born sons of the Egyptians. After that, Pharaoh agrees to let the descendants of Isaac leave Egypt. Pharaoh then pursues Moses until Jehovah opens up a road through the Red Sea, allowing the Israelites to pass through and swallowing up Pharaoh's charioteers.

The Children of Israel follow Moses' old route toward Midian until they stop at Mt. Sinai. When Reuel hears that Moses is close by, he comes to meet him, bringing Moses' wife and two sons with him. Moses goes out to meet him, bows down and kisses him. After the prolonged desert greeting, they go into Moses' tent.

Moses tells his father-in-law about everything Jehovah has done to Pharaoh and the Egyptians for Israel's sake, about all the hardships they met along the way and how Jehovah saved them. Reuel is delighted to hear it.

"Praise be to Jehovah who has rescued you from Pharaoh and the Egyptians. Now I know that the God of Abraham is greater than all other gods!"

Grabbing Moses by the hand, Reuel moves slowly from the tent toward the altar that Moses has built in the center of the camp. Together, they offer a burnt offering and other sacrifices to Jehovah. Then, Moses invites his brother, Aaron, with all the elders of Israel to eat bread with them in the presence of Jehovah.

Afterwards, as Reuel watches Moses work, he offers some advice. "What is this you are doing for the people? Why are you the only judge, while all these people stand around waiting for you from morning till evening?"

"Because the people come to me to seek Jehovah's will," answers Moses. "Whenever they have a dispute, it is brought to me, and I decide between the parties and inform them of Jehovah's decrees and laws."

"What you're doing isn't good," replies Reuel. "You and these people who come to you will only wear yourselves out. The work is too heavy for you. You can't handle it alone. Listen, I'll give you some advice, and may Jehovah be with you. You must be the people's representative before Jehovah and bring their disputes to him. Teach them the decrees and laws, and show them the way to live and the duties they are to perform.

"But select capable men from all the people—men who fear Jehovah, trustworthy men who aren't corrupt—and appoint them as officials over thousands, hundreds, fifties and tens. Have them serve as judges for the people, but have them bring every difficult case to you. The simple cases they can decide themselves. That will make your load lighter. If you do this —and Jehovah so commands—you will be able to stand the strain, and all these people will go home satisfied."

Moses listens to his father-in-law's advice and does everything he says. After a few days, Reuel returns to his own people, the Children of the East. Reuel's son, Hobab, however, decides to stay on with Moses.

After receiving the ten commandments, building the Tabernacle and installing the Ark of the Covenant, Moses prepares to set out from Mount Sinai. Before leaving, he approaches his brother-in-law, Hobab.

"We are setting out for the place Jehovah promised us. Come with us and we'll treat you well, for the God of Abraham has promised good things to both Isaac and Ishmael."

"Sorry," answers Hobab. "I'm going back to my own land and my own people."

"Please don't leave us," Moses insists. "You know where we should camp in the desert, and you can be our eyes. If you come with us, we will share with you whatever good things Jehovah gives us."

So Hobab, the Bedouin, becomes the guide for the Children of Israel in their wanderings in the desert and his descendants live with the Hebrews from that time on instead of returning to the Children of the East.

At about the same time, another of the Children of the East, a man named Jephunneh the Kenizzite, a descendant of Jacob's brother Esau, is adopted into the tribe of Judah along with his son, a man with the Arabic name Caleb.

Meanwhile, as the Israelites approach the promised land, their enemies send a delegation to a prophet of Jehovah named Balaam to get his advice on how to deal with the intruders...

Balaam

The oracle of Balaam son of Beor,
the oracle of one whose eye sees clearly,
the oracle of one who hears the words of God,
who has knowledge from the Most High,
who sees a vision from the Almighty,
who falls prostrate, and whose eyes are opened:
"I see him, but not now;
I behold him, but not near.
A star will come out of Jacob;
A scepter will rise out of Israel."

Numbers 24:15-17 (NIV)

"And recite to them the story of the person
Whom Our revelations were given to him,
But he removed himself from them,
And thus the devil followed him,
And He became of those who went astray."

Qur'an 7:175

Balaam is alone with his thoughts. The others give him plenty of distance, a sign of respect. After all, this is the reason they have come such a long distance twice over the last two weeks. They are now about half way to their destination. The caravan left Pethor and the Euphrates River three days ago and despite the rugged terrain they have made good time.

While Balaam rides ahead on his donkey, the rest follow on camel or on foot. Balaam has had plenty of time to think over the past few days and while the trip is uncomfortable, he has a strange feeling that this might be the most important thing he will ever do. He is well known in

Mesopotamia and has been receiving messages and visions from Jehovah since he was a teenager.

The first vision came shortly after the Ishmaelite traders left. Balaam had been hired by the owner of the roadside inn to help clean out the stables after the different caravans departed. It was a dirty and thankless job, but as an orphan, Balaam couldn't be choosy about his employment. It was enough to keep him from starving. Besides, he got to hear a lot of stories and keep up on the news from the outside world brought in by the different nomads and merchants.

Balaam remembers well that night, sitting around the fire listening to the Ishmaelites tell their tall tales. Most of them were entertaining, but he couldn't take them too seriously. One story, however, dug into his soul and burned like a fire. He would later recognize it as the first time Jehovah spoke directly to him to reveal the truth about himself, the God of Abraham.

It was the story of a boy about Balaam's age who was sold as a slave by his brothers. The great grandpa of the hardened Bedouin relating the story had been the one to accompany the lad all the way to Egypt. The young man's name was Joseph. He told how his ancestor had become attached to the boy but was constrained by financial difficulties to sell him. However, he had ensured that Joseph got sold to a good man, the chief of Pharaoh's guard.

He then related how, after being accused of attempted rape by the chief's wife and thrown in prison, Joseph was able to interpret dreams with the help of his God. Later on, this gift from the one true God allowed Joseph to interpret Pharaoh's dream. Soon after, not only was Joseph released from prison, he was promoted to Prime Minister of Egypt.

Balaam listened spellbound as the traders continued to relate how Joseph saved the entire region of Mesopotamia during the infamous seven-year famine. Joseph had stocked grain during the seven years before the famine so he had enough in reserve not only to feed the Egyptians, but also his own family from Canaan and everyone else looking to fend off starvation.

As Balaam stood leaning against the rough wood of the stable in the dim light of that fire lit night, he felt a strange warmth spread over his body. He sensed a deep desire to know this Jehovah, the God of Joseph. Over the next few days, he spent all the time he could with the Ishmaelites, learning all the stories of their God. He learned about the Creation of the world, Noah and the flood, Abraham and the covenant, Ishmael, Isaac, Jacob, and Esau. He also heard the rumors of strange things happening in Egypt; of a man named Moses and the miracles he was performing in the name of Jehovah. He heard unbelievable rumors of water turning to blood; of plagues of frogs, and flies and boils; and of Pharaoh's unwillingness to recognize the power of Jehovah.

Balaam started praying to Jehovah in the stillness of the night when his work was done and everyone was asleep. It was just him, the stars and the real presence of Jehovah. After a while, people started noticing that Balaam seemed to know things others didn't and could predict the future. Caravans that received his blessings met with greater success than normal. Soon, Balaam quit his job at the stables, as these merchants were more than willing to give him gifts in order to hear whatever message he had from this invisible God.

Because of the nature of his clients' work, Balaam's reputation soon spread throughout all the routes traveled by the Ishmaelite and Midianite traders. From Arabia to Chaldea to Egypt and all across Mesopotamia, he was known as a prophet who knew *Izmul Azam* as the Arabs called the powerful name of God, the name that when pronounced could alter one's destiny.

An extra sharp jolt from his donkey brings Balaam back to the present. As he bounces along to the rhythm of the donkey's swaying back, he can't help but feel that this is his most important mission ever. Otherwise, he would never have agreed to come the 400 miles from his home on the Euphrates River to the God-forsaken deserts of northern Arabia. *How did I end up on this road?* His thoughts drift back...

The emissaries from King Balak arrived in the middle of the night, which didn't stop them from pounding on Balaam's door and waking him out of a deep sleep. They informed him that they were some of the top officials of Moab and Midian and that they were menaced by a vast horde of people coming out of Egypt.

Balaam instantly felt in his spirit that it must be the people of Joseph that had finally escaped from Egypt. Maybe Moses and his miracles from Jehovah had finally convinced Pharaoh to let them go. He had heard rumors the last few years of a miraculous crossing of the Red Sea and a huge group of nomads, numbering in the millions, wandering around the deserts of the Sinai Peninsula.

But these were important people, obviously, and Balaam didn't want to offend them so he invited them in.

"Stay here overnight," Balaam said, "and I'll tell you in the morning whatever Jehovah directs me to say."

That night, Jehovah came to Balaam and asked him, "Who are these men?"

"They have come from King Balak of Moab," he replied. "The king says that a vast horde of people from Egypt has arrived at his border, and he wants me to go at once and curse them, in the hope that he can battle them successfully."

"Don't do it!" Jehovah told Balaam. "You are not to curse them, for I have blessed them!"

So, the next morning, Balaam told the men, "Go on home! Jehovah won't let me do it."

King Balak didn't give up very easily, however. A few weeks later, the ambassadors were back with even more important officials making up the delegation.

"King Balak pleads with you to come," they insisted. "He promises you great honors plus any payment you ask. Name your own figure! Only come and curse these people for us."

But Balaam replied, "If he were to give me a palace filled with silver and gold, I could do nothing contrary to the command of Jehovah, my God. However, stay here tonight so that I can find out whether Jehovah will add anything to what he said before."

That night Jehovah told Balaam, "Get up and go with these men, but be sure to say only what I tell you to."

So here he is, on his donkey traveling hundreds of miles to hopefully make himself very rich and increase his reputation even more. He is a little nervous, though. He knows he can only say what Jehovah tells him to and he's afraid that might not be what Balak wants to hear. Maybe he won't make much for himself after all. If only there was a way around it. *Can I somehow trick Jehovah? It seems far fetched, but...*

Suddenly, Balaam is jerked to the side as his normally passive donkey jumps sideways into the ditch. Balaam tumbles off to the side and bruises his elbow on some rocks on the other side of the ditch. Furious, he picks himself up, brushes himself off and starts beating the stupid animal with his cane. He finally persuades the stubborn beast to get back on the road, and Balaam gingerly remounts.

A few hundred feet later, as they pass a vineyard between two walls, the donkey again tries to bolt. This time, she crushes Balaam's foot between her fat little belly and the wall. Howling in pain, Balaam again gives the good-for-nothing animal some vicious swats on the top of the head until she once again starts to move forward.

Balaam can't figure it out. The ass has never caused him any difficulty before. What possesses her now? He is completely awakened out of his reverie now and is paying close attention to just moving forward without getting hurt. Things go okay for a couple of miles until they come to a narrow part of the path between two steep cliffs. There's barely enough room for one donkey or one camel to pass.

This time, the donkey just stops on a dime and sits down. No matter how much Balaam beats her, she refuses to move. Finally, the ass looks up at Balaam, opens her mouth and speaks!

"What have I done that deserves your beating me these three times?" She demands.

"Because you have made me look like a fool!" Balaam shouts without thinking. "I wish I had a sword with me, I'd kill you!"

"Have I ever done anything like this before in my entire life?" The donkey continues.

"No," Balaam admits.

Suddenly, Balaam sees an angel standing right in front of him with a drawn sword of fire. The being is so bright, Balaam falls on his face to the ground, his eyes closed to keep from being blinded.

"Why did you beat your donkey those three times?" the angel demanded. "I have come to stop you because you are headed for destruction. Three times the donkey saw me and shied away from me; otherwise I would certainly have killed you by now, and spared her."

Then Balaam confesses, "I have sinned. I didn't realize you were there. I will go back home if you don't want me to go on."

But the angel tells him, "Go with the men, but say only what I tell you to say."

So, Balaam continues on with his donkey and the caravan until they came to the Arnon River where they meet King Balak who greets him, wondering why he's taken so long.

"I've come, but I warn you, I can't say anything except what Jehovah tells me to say." Balaam doesn't mention anything about the embarrassing incident with the donkey.

The next morning, Balaam, Balak and the rest of the delegation climb to the top of Mount Bamoth-Baal where they can see the Israelite camp spread out below them. There they build seven altars and sacrifice a bull and a ram on each altar.

"Wait for me here by the altars," Balaam tells Balak and the rest. "I'll go see if Jehovah will meet with me. I'll let you know what He says."

Balaam heads further up the peak until he's in a completely isolated cleft overlooking the valley below. There, Jehovah meets with him and gives him a message for Balak.

Balaam goes back down to where the others are eagerly waiting and gives them the message from Jehovah.

"King Balak has brought me from the land of Aram, from the eastern mountains to curse the Hebrews. But how can I curse what Jehovah has not cursed? How can I denounce a people Jehovah has not denounced? If only I could die as happy as an Israelite!"

Balak is furious. "I told you to curse my enemies and you've blessed them!"

But Balaam replies, "Can I say anything except what Jehovah tells me to?"

So Balak tries again. They all go up to the top of Mount Pisgah and offer seven more sacrifices just like the first time. Once again, Balaam goes off by himself and Jehovah meets him and gives him a message.

"What has Jehovah said?" Balak inquires eagerly when Balaam comes back.

Balaam looks Balak in the eye and responds, "Jehovah is not a man that he should lie. He doesn't change his mind like humans do. Has he ever promised something without doing it?

"Look, I've received a command to bless them, for Jehovah has blessed them, and I cannot reverse it! Jehovah their God is with them. He is their King!"

"If you're not going to curse them, at least don't bless them!" Balak exclaims in shock.

"Didn't I tell you that I must say whatever Jehovah tells me to?"

Balak still hasn't given up, so they try again from the top of Mount Peor, overlooking the desert. This time, Balaam doesn't bother going off by himself to meet Jehovah. He knows Jehovah is going to bless Israel. So he goes immediately to look out over the Israeli camp spread out over the plain neatly divided by tribal areas.

The Spirit of Jehovah comes upon Balaam and he prophesies.

"I have listened to the word of Jehovah. I have seen what the Ruler of All showed me. I fell, and my eyes were opened. Oh, the joys awaiting Israel! I see them spread before me as green valleys, and fruitful gardens by the riverside; as aloes planted by Jehovah himself; as cedar trees beside the waters.

"They shall be blessed and they shall live in many places. Their kingdom is exalted. Blessed is everyone who blesses you, O Israel, and curses shall fall upon everyone who curses you."

Balak is livid with rage. Striking his hands together in anger and disgust he shouts, "I called you to curse my enemies and instead you have blessed them three times!

"Get out of here! Go back home! I had planned to promote you to great honor, but Jehovah has kept you from it!"

Balaam replies, "Didn't I tell your messengers that even if you gave me a palace filled with silver and gold, I couldn't go beyond the words of

Jehovah, and could not say a word of my own? I said that I would say only what Jehovah says!

"Yes, I'll go back to my own people now. But first, let me tell you what Israel's going to do to your people!"

With that introduction, Balaam proceeds to give a prophecy of the future arrival of a deliverer, called the *Meshicha* by the Jews.

"I see him, but not now. I see him, but not near. A star will come out of Jacob. A scepter will rise out of Israel."

With that, Balaam leaves for Pethor. But not before giving some of his own advice to Balak on how to get the Israelites out of favor with Jehovah. Following Balaam's advice, Balak sends in a bunch of wild, young party girls into the Israeli camp and seduces many of the Hebrew men. In the end, the girls even draw many of the men into worshipping their own local gods.

So, Balaam was a prophet of Jehovah and even predicted the coming of the *Meshicha*. But he ends up being killed along with the rest of King Balak's army when Moses and those faithful to Jehovah attack and destroy those who have fallen back into idolatry.

Meanwhile, out in the deserts of Arabia, a man named Job is about to have an extraordinary encounter with the supernatural...

Job

There was a man in the land of Uz
Whose name was Job
That man was blameless and upright
And one who feared God
And turned away from evil...
This man was the greatest
Of all the children of the east.

Job 1:1-3

And then there was Job: when he called to his Lord,
"Adversity has come upon me,
And You are the most merciful of the merciful,"
We answered him, and removed the adversity affecting him;
And We gave him back his kin,
Plus an equal number besides, as a mercy from Us,
And a reminder for the devoted.

Qur'an 21:83-84

Job wakes up in a cold sweat. It's still dark outside the partially opened door of his tent. A cool desert breeze blows in and kicks up some dust in the corner as the first traces of dawn redden the eastern horizon. He rolls over on his back and takes a few deep breaths as he tries to calm his pounding heart.

It's the same nightmare all over again and just as terrifying as the first time. Job isn't used to remembering his dreams, but this one was so vivid he can remember it to the last detail. Maybe Jehovah is trying to send him some kind of warning.

The dream starts off pleasant enough. Job finds himself soaring out of his tent and up into the air, through the clouds and into a light so bright he is temporarily blinded. When his eyes adjust, he realizes he is in a wood, bright with the green of spring and filled with multicolored birds flitting back and forth, singing in all different pitches and melodies, somehow harmonizing into a magnificent chorus.

In the next instant, Job is in a different place. The scenery changes in a moment from pastoral to urban: a city, glowing with gold, silver and precious stones. Suddenly, he is in the presence of Jehovah. He doesn't see Jehovah, but he somehow feels that over there, just out of view no matter where he turns, is the very essence of Jehovah.

Job hits the ground prostrate, wondering if his life's about to be over. At the same time, he feels no fear, only an overwhelming sensation of love and compassion. It is like eyes are boring into him, begging him to understand something, something very important.

Suddenly, an icy wind whips into the room and chills him to the bone as the hair stands up on his arms. Afraid to turn around, yet compelled to, Job sees a dark thing slink into the crowd of radiant beings gathered in front of Jehovah. The creature has the form of a heavily muscled man with smooth, pale skin and piercing blue eyes like a deep, icy sea.

The voice of Jehovah seeps softly and powerfully into his mind. Yet it isn't Job he speaks to, but rather the cold stranger.

"Where do you come from, friend?"

Job feels, rather then sees all eyes turn to the newcomer.

"From wandering this way and that on the earth," he replies in an expressionless monotone. "And walking about on it."

Job hears whispering among the angels. As often happens in dreams, he is able to actually hear the words as they slowly come into focus from a thousand voices all around him.

"Is it really?..."

"Does he dare?"

"Yep, it's the rebel all right."

"The Accuser?"

"Yeah, Satan himself."

Jehovah's voice silences the whispering, remaining soothing, yet strong. "Have you taken note of my servant Job? For there is no one like him on earth, a man without sin and upright, fearing Jehovah and keeping himself far from evil."

Job swallows hard. While he feels that he does know and try to serve Jehovah, he can't believe Jehovah himself would say such things about him. He feels his very being drawn by what he can only describe as an irresistible love.

"Is it for nothing that Job is a god-fearing man?" Satan's icy voice cuts through the air like a knife. "Have you yourself not put a wall round him and his house and all he has on every side, blessing the work of his hands, and increasing his cattle in the land? But now, put out your hand against all he has, and he will curse you to your face."

Jehovah's reply hits Job like a load of bricks as his heart sinks. "Very well, then," Jehovah says to Satan. "I give all he has into your hands, only do not put a finger on the man himself."

And that's when Job wakes up in a cold sweat. He's had the same dream every night for the last six days. Today is the seventh. *What can it mean? Is it a warning? What am I supposed to do with it all anyway?*

Job decides to get up. He steps outside the tent and dips his hands in the water jar. He slowly and methodically washes his face, head, hands and feet and then moves to the top of the hill under the acacia tree where he usually says his morning prayers. He rolls out his mat and begins to talk to Jehovah, prostrate before him as he faces the rising sun.

His prayers finished, Job sits cross-legged on the mat and reflects on his past and how Jehovah has brought him to this point in his life. One of Job's grandsons comes out and sits on his lap.

"Gram-pa..." the boy looks up into Job's face. "Tell me some stories."

"Okay, let me see..." Job stares off into the distance. "My great-great grandfather was the patriarch, Esau, brother of Jacob, son of Isaac and grandson of Abraham. One day, Esau came back to the camp hungry just as Jacob was finishing cooking a bowl of lentils. Jacob convinced Esau to sell him his birthright for that bowl of soup. Later on, when Isaac was about to die..."

"What does that mean," interrupts the child. "To die?"

"Well, it's kind of like when you go into a long sleep and don't wake up for a long time. Anyway, so Jacob pretended to be Esau by tying sheep skins on his arms because Esau was really hairy..."

"Kind uh like you, huh, Gram-pa?"

"Yeah, kind of like me. So Jacob got the blessing that Isaac meant for Esau. Esau was upset, so Jacob fled during the night. Jacob lived with his Uncle Laban and married his two daughters, Rachel and Leah. Jacob wanted to be friends again with his brother so they got together and made peace. But even though Esau forgave Jacob, he didn't trust him, so he moved his family to...you see that mountain over there?"

Job points to an impressive summit in the distance as his grandson follows his finger with his eyes. "Yeah, I see it...what's its name?"

"That, my boy, is Mount Seir. That's where we started to be called the Edomites and that's where Esau met my great-great grandmother

Basemath, who was the daughter of your great-great-great-great-grandfather Abraham's son Ishmael…"

"That's confusing…."

"Yeah, but one day you'll learn all the names of our ancestors, like my dad Zerah and my grandpa Reuel. But anyway, one of the most important stories is about Abraham coming to visit Ishmael here in the desert. Ishmael was living near the well of *Zamzam* in the town of *Makkah*. Abraham had visited several other times, but this time, he and Ishmael built an altar to Jehovah there in *Makkah*. They walled it off so the animals wouldn't defile it. Abraham wanted to make sure we never forgot about Jehovah, the one who created us and delivered our ancestors from our enemies so many times. So that's why we make a pilgrimage there every year."

"When am I going to get to go…?"

"There, there, all in good time. Let's see, there's some other interesting stories…have I told you about our first king, Balaam son of Beor?"

"You mean the guy who talked to his donkey?"

"Yep, that's the one. Remember, he was a true prophet of Jehovah at one point. But he made some bad choices. He liked money a lot so he helped the enemies of our cousins the Israelites. By sending some bad women into the Israelite camp he made them forget about our God, Jehovah, and worship idols, like Baal. Finally, the Israelites recognized their mistake and when they fought to regain their freedom, King Balaam was killed."

"So did he go to sleep, too…?"

"Yep, that's right. Good for you. So that's how I became king. Balaam didn't have any children so our clan had to elect a new king and they chose me. I suppose they think I'm okay at solving their problems. I certainly don't get caught up in all their little feuds and gossiping…"

"What's a feud? What's gossiping?"

"Never mind…you'll learn soon enough, unfortunately…" Job's voice trails off as he sees a rider approaching in the distance in a cloud of dust.

"Peace be upon you, father!" the man cries as he grabs Job's outstretched hand in vise-like grip. "I was watching the oxen and the donkeys out in the fields when a group of bandits attacked us. They killed all the others…I'm the only one who has escaped to tell you!"

Almost immediately, another messenger comes running up shouting, "There was a huge thunderstorm last night and lightening was everywhere. It burned up your sheep and the other shepherds! I'm the only one left!"

As the shepherd falls sobbing to the ground in exhaustion, another man comes rushing up. "Three raiding parties of nomads swept down on your camels and carried them off. They massacred all your servants…I barely escaped to tell you!"

Yet another servant comes riding up breathless on a horse. "Your sons and daughters were feasting at the oldest brother's house," he gasps. "Suddenly a tornado swooped in from the desert and struck the house. It collapsed on them and they are dead, and I am the only one who has survived to tell you!"

Devastated, Job stumbles to his feet, tears his robe, rips off his turban and calls for his servant to shave his head. Falling to the ground in the midst of the hair clippings, Job worships. "With nothing I came out of my mother's body, and with nothing I will go back there. Jehovah gave and Jehovah has taken away. Let Jehovah's name be praised."

That night, after crying himself to sleep, Job has another dream. This one starts in the same way, but ends differently. Once again he is transported to Paradise into the very presence of Jehovah where Satan has come again.

"Where do you come from, my friend?" Jehovah again asks Satan.

"From wandering this way and that on the earth," Satan replies. "And walking about on it."

"Have you taken note of my servant Job?" Jehovah continues. "For there is no one like him on earth, a man without sin and upright, fearing Jehovah and keeping himself far from evil. And he still keeps his righteousness, though you have been moving me to send destruction on him without cause."

"Skin for skin!" Satan retorts. "All a man has he will give for his life. But now, if you only put your hand on his bone and his flesh, he will certainly curse you to your face."

"I place him in your hands," Jehovah says with boundless love in his voice. "Only do not take his life."

Job then sees Satan coming directly toward him with hatred gleaming in his eyes. The Devil bends down, picks up some dust and casts it over Job's body. As the dust hits his skin, Job sees sores erupt all over as pain shoots up to his brain and his whole body convulses in agony.

Job again wakes up in a cold sweat. *Whew! It was only a dream…or was it?* The pain is still there. Job slowly lifts up the sheep skins covering his body from the early morning chill and immediately closes his eyes. His body is covered with weeping, draining boils.

Using the knowledge of medicine passed down from his great-great grandmother, Basemath, Job covers the wounds in ashes and charcoal from the fire. He tries to lance the abscesses with a sharp piece of pottery. As he lies in misery by the embers of the evening fire, his wife comes out and joins him. Looking down at his sickly body, she gives a gasp and pulls back.

"Are you still keeping your faith in Jehovah? Curse him, and put an end to yourself."

"You are talking like a fool," Job mutters between teeth clenched in suffering. "If we take the good that Jehovah sends us, shouldn't we take the evil as well?"

Three of Job's friends, Eliphaz the Temanite, Bildad the Shuhite and Zophar the Naamathite, hear about all the troubles that have come upon him. They get together and decide to go visit Job to see if they can comfort him. When they see him from a distance, they hardly recognize him. Weeping, they tear their robes and sprinkle dust on their heads in mourning. Then they sit on the ground with him for seven days and seven nights. No one says a word, because they see how great his suffering is.

On the eighth day, Job breaks the silence. "Why wasn't I stillborn? Then I'd be in peace. I want to die, but death won't come.

"You know," replies Eliphaz. "You've helped so many people. But now you're touched by problems and your mind is troubled. Isn't Jehovah your support, and your upright life your hope?

"Have you ever seen destruction come on an upright man? People reap what they sow. Stick with Jehovah. After punishing, he comforts. After wounding, he heals."

"If only Jehovah would answer my prayer!" Job responds. "If only he would put an end to me and cut off! Then, I would be comforted. So now you see my sad condition and are afraid. Teach me and I will be quiet. Make me see my error and I'll repent.

"When I go to bed, I think, *When will it be time to get up?* But the night is long, and I toss and turn till morning. My body is wasting away. I have no hope.

"Remember, O Jehovah," Job continues as he lifts up his hands in prayer. "That my life is nothing. I will not keep quiet. I will cry bitterly. I have terrible dreams and nightmares. A hard death seems better to me than my pain.

"What is man, O Jehovah, that you pay attention to him? Why do you test him every minute? If I've done wrong, let me know!"

"Job, how long will you say these things?" interjects Bildad. "Does Jehovah make mistakes? If you are so upright, he'll certainly clear your name. We don't know anything, because our days on earth are like a shadow. Surely, Jehovah won't reject him who is pure in heart."

"True...," Job admits. "But how is it possible for a man to get right before Jehovah? He is wise and powerful. He does great things and wonders without number.

"He goes past me and I see nothing. If he wants to take something, who can refuse him? Who may say to him, *What are you doing?*

"How much less may I answer him. Even if my cause was good, I would not be able to give an appropriate response. I can only ask him for grace. I have done no wrong. I don't care anymore what becomes of me. I'm tired of life. It's all the same to me. He puts an end to the evil and the good together.

"Don't reject me, Jehovah," Job prays again. "Make clear to me what you have against me. You made me. But then you destroyed me. But despite all this, you have been kind to me. Your grace has been with me, and you've kept my spirit safe."

"Is no one going to answer you, Job?" says Zophar in surprise. "Are you going to get away with this mockery? You may say you've done nothing wrong, but if Jehovah would make it clear to you, you'd realize your error."

"No doubt you know everything, and all wisdom ends with you!" Job bursts out sarcastically. "But I have a mind as well as you. I am equal to you. Who *doesn't* know such things?

"But keep on making fun of me. Everyone's life is in Jehovah's hands. He has wisdom and strength. Power and knowledge are his. He reveals the deep things of darkness. He makes nations great, and destroys them. But I want to talk to Jehovah face to face.

"But you, my friends, haven't said anything worthwhile yet! If only you would keep quiet! It would make me think you had a little wisdom at least! Listen to me!

"Though Jehovah kill me, yet I will trust him. I won't stop asking him for answers. This is my hope because only a friend would dare to come before him! Now I have put my case in order, and I am certain that I will be seen to be right.

"I only ask two things of you," Job again addresses Jehovah directly. "Stop this pain and help me to not be afraid of you. Then when I hear you, I'll answer. Let me present my case before you.

"Man dies and is gone. He gives up his spirit, and where is he? Till the end of time, the dead won't awaken or come out of their sleep. How I long for that rest!"

"Can anyone argue with such useless statements?" interrupts Eliphaz. "Seriously, Job, it seems like you have no fear of Jehovah at all. It's by your words that you are judged to be in the wrong, and not by me."

"Some comforters you are!" says Job, shaking his head. "I would never say such things if I was in your place. Instead I would strengthen and comfort you with my words.

"My spirit is broken. My days are ended. The grave is waiting for me. Where is my hope? Are we to go down together into the dust?"

"How long will it be before you are done talking?" Bildad sighs. "Get some wisdom, and it will be worth our while to say what is on our minds. Why do you treat us like dogs?"

"I give a cry for help," Job spurts out. "But no one takes up my cause. Jehovah breaks me down and I am gone. He uproots my hope like a tree.

"Have pity on me, O my friends, for the hand of Jehovah is heavy on me. But I am certain that my Redeemer lives, and that in the end he will take his stand on the earth. Then, I will see Jehovah. I myself will see him. How I long for that day!"

"What you say troubles me," interjects Zophar. "Your arguments shame me and your answers to me are without wisdom. There is no peace for rich people like you. You never have enough. You always want more. Even if you became more wealthy, you'd never be satisfied."

"Let me speak my mind," answers Job. "After that, go on making fun of me. Is my complaint against mere men? I tremble inside at what I'm about to say.

"Why do the wicked live long lives? Why do they become old and powerful? They are free from fear and they die in peace. Yet they are nothing but rebels against the Ruler of All and want nothing to do with him. The good and the bad go down together to the dust and are no more. Yet you try and comfort me with such useless words!"

"Do you really think that Jehovah has use of you?" says Eliphaz. "Is it because you honor him that he's brought all this on you? Make peace with Jehovah and all will be well. Repent and pray to him, and he will answer."

"If only I knew where Jehovah was!" Job cries out. "I would present my case before him. He would pay attention to me. There, an upright man might get an honest hearing! But, wherever I go, forward, backward, right or left, I can't find him!

"My only hope is that after I have been tested, I will come out as gold. My feet have followed Jehovah's steps. I have turned neither to the left or the right. I have stored up Jehovah's words in my heart."

"Everything belongs to Jehovah," interrupts Bildad. "How is it possible for a man to be upright before him?"

"If only I could live my life over again. All was well in the past. When I went into town I was respected by all. I helped the poor, widows and orphans. I was a chief among my people and king over all the land.

"But now those who are younger than I make fun of me. I am shameful and disgusting to them. They stay far away from me. I am afraid and my hope is gone like the wind. My pain never goes away. I have become like dust.

"I vowed not to look lustfully at a girl. If my heart gave in to lust, or if I stole someone's property, or if my heart went after another man's wife, or if I treated my servants harshly, what could I say to Jehovah when I stand before him to be judged? What answer might I give to his questions?"

With Job's final words, all four of the older men sit silently, each lost in his own thoughts. Suddenly, a gust of wind stirs up the leaves scattered about under the tree and whips the men's turbans around their faces. The sky grows dark as lightning flashes in the distance around Mount Seir. Across the desert, dust devils spin out of control like whirling dervishes. A few raindrops spatter rhythmically on the canvas of Job's tent as the four men seek out shelter. Before they can get inside, though, a gentle voice swoops out of the sky and surrounds them in its embrace. They all fall face down in fear as they recognize the presence of Jehovah.

"Who is this who dares question Jehovah? Face me like a man and answer me.

"Where were you when I laid the foundation of the earth? Tell me, if you know. Who put down its cornerstone—when the morning stars made songs together and all the sons of the gods gave cries of joy?

"Where were you when the sea came to birth, and I said to it *So far you may come and no farther*? Have you ever ordered the dawn to come forth? Have you walked in the secret places of the deep? Have the doors of death been open to you?

"Do you know where light and darkness are or where they come from? No doubt you know, for by then you were already born, and you've already lived so long! Do you know where the storehouses of wind, rain, thunder and lightening are?

"Who is this who pretends to teach the Ruler of All? You wanted an audience, here it is. Present your case before me!"

In the heavy silence that descends like the eye of the storm, Job's muffled voice answers from the ground.

"What answer can I give to you? I'm putting my hand over my mouth. I've said what was on my mind, but I won't do it again."

Just as quickly as the calm descended, the storm picks up its fury again as Jehovah's voice continues:

"Get your strength together and face me like a man. Do you give strength to the horse? Is it by your hand that his neck is so powerful? He laughs at fear. He goes out clothed in his strength. Shaking with passion, he is not able to keep quiet at the sound of the horn.

"Is it through your knowledge that the hawk takes his flight, stretching out his wings to the south? Is it by your orders that the eagle goes up and makes his resting-place on high?

"I made the hippopotamus just like I made you. He eats grass like a cow. He is strong and powerful. He rests under the trees of the river and in the pool under the shade of the water plants. Nothing frightens him. He is master of his territory and defends it well. Is it you who made him?

"Who ever went against me, and got the better of me? There is no one under heaven!"

As quickly as the storm came, it disappears leaving behind a cool, refreshing breeze scented with eucalyptus. Sensing that Jehovah has not left yet, Job slowly raises his head and speaks again.

"I see that you are able to do everything. I have been talking senselessly about wonders too great for my understanding. I'd heard of you, but now I've seen you. So I testify that what I said is false. I repent in sorrow, my face to the dust."

Job bows down to the ground as the still small voice of Jehovah speaks again.

"Eliphaz, I am very angry with you and your two friends, because you have not said what is right about me, as my friend Job has. So now go to my friend Job and he will pray for you, so I won't punish you. You have not said what is right about me as Job has."

So Eliphaz, Bildad and Zophar do what Jehovah tells them. After Job prays for his friends, Jehovah heals him and makes him even more prosperous giving him twice as much as he had before. All his family and friends come to celebrate with him at his new house. They comfort and console him over all the trouble that has come upon him.

Jehovah blesses the second part of Job's life more than the first. He gets 14,000 sheep, 6,000 camels, 1,000 yoke of oxen and 1,000 donkeys. And he also has seven sons and three daughters. Everyone agrees that they are the most beautiful women in all the land. Their father gives them an inheritance along with their brothers.

After this, Job lives 140 years. He sees his children and their children to the fourth generation. And so he dies, old and full of years, the greatest of the Children of the East.

Before Job's death, though, a group of nomads prepares to enter the land of Canaan, led by an old Arab named Caleb, the son of Jephunneh the Kenizzite...

Caleb & Joshua

...So here I [Caleb] am today,
Eighty-five years old!
I am still as strong today
As the day Moses sent me out
I'm just as vigorous to go out to battle
Now as I was then.

Joshua 14:10-11 (NIV)

Moses said...enter the holy land...
They said, "Moses, there is in fact
A nation of giants there...
Two God-blessed men
Among those in dread said,
"Enter the gate in spite of them;
Once you get in you will prevail.
But let your trust be reposed in God,
If you are believers."

Qur'an 5:20-23

As he rounds the top of the hill, Caleb pauses to catch his breath. Climbing mountains isn't getting any easier at 85 years old. Shielding his intense steel gray eyes against the setting sun, he looks back at the others. Although half his age, the rest of his men are several hundred yards back and struggling to make it up the slope. Caleb's curly black hair hangs loosely over his forehead and down to his shoulders and is just starting to get streaked with a little silver. His full beard is black except for a startling white streak that runs from under his lower lip, down his chin and off to the tip of his goatee. It makes him look like he has a skunk attached to the front of his face.

Caleb's face is wrinkled and tanned like leather from 40 years wandering in the desert. Despite his age, his body stands erect and his muscles lithe and taut, like a leopard crouched and ready to strike. Looking back at his men, Caleb can't help but smile and remember what he just told Joshua yesterday.

Here I am today, 85 years old! I am still as strong today as the day Moses sent me out 40 years ago to spy out the land. I'm just as vigorous and ready for battle now as I was then.

The memories warm Caleb's heart as he patiently waits for the others. It has been a long time, but he remembers the last time he crowned this hill as if it was yesterday. He was in the prime of life and was accompanied by his best friend Joshua Bar Nun...

"Hey, Caleb!" Joshua shouted back toward Caleb who was just then coming up the last steep stretch before the summit. "You're not going to believe this!"

Caleb pulled to a stop next to Joshua and followed his finger pointing to the top of the next ridge. A massive stone fortress hung precariously to the cliffs with the only access a narrow path winding up the crest from the valley below. Terraced up from the rippling brook at the bottom were row upon row of vines heavy with fruit. Even from this distance, Caleb could tell that these grapes were extraordinary. He'd never seen clusters that big!

They spent several days wandering around the town, gathering information from the peasants working the vineyards. They kept a low profile, sleeping under bushes and eating just what they could glean from the fields and what wild plants they recognized as edible. The land was obviously rich and wild berries, fruits and nuts were in abundance.

They spent many a night under the stars in silence or silently recounting the tales they had heard growing up about the great God of Abraham. Joshua knew mostly the recent stories of Moses and Aaron and the plagues in Egypt and the crossing of the Red Sea. He also told Caleb about his time up on Mount Sinai with Moses and Jehovah where they spent 40 days fasting. Finally, Jehovah himself had appeared to Moses and proclaimed himself in words that Joshua had quickly memorized and never forgot as he repeated them to himself many times throughout the day as part of his prayers.

Jehovah, Jehovah, a merciful and gracious God, slow to anger, and abundant in loving kindness and truth, keeping loving kindness for thousands, forgiving iniquity and disobedience and sin...

Caleb, on the other hand, had joined the Hebrews just after Sinai. His father, Jephunneh, was a Kenizzite. Their ancestor was Kenaz, one of the clans of Esau, Jacob's brother. So Caleb related to Joshua the tales he had grown up hearing in the East: stories of Abraham, Ishmael, Midian, Joseph, Jethro, Balaam and Job.

Caleb told Joshua how he had accompanied Jethro when he came to visit Moses at Mount Sinai and was fascinated with the idea of the sanctuary Moses had built. This was a place where Jehovah, the God of Abraham from all his childhood stories, came and talked to Moses face to face. At the time, Caleb was really seeking for a more personal encounter with the God of his ancestors so he decided to bind himself to the tribe of Israel and had been adopted in as a member of the clan of Judah.

Now, both Caleb and Joshua found themselves outside a Canaanite castle in the town of Kiriath Arba, spying out the land. From a human point of view, things were pretty discouraging. The men of Kiriath Arba were giants, descendants of the Nephilim. They had also discovered that the region was inhabited by a group of three giants, Ahiman, Sheshai and Talmai, who were renowned warriors and the sons of one of the most infamous men since the time of the flood, Anak himself.

After they had scouted out the rest of that part of the Negev Desert, they went down into the valley by Kiriath Arba, called Eschol, and cut off one of the huge clusters of grapes to take back as evidence of the richness of the land. The fruit was so massive that it was all Joshua and Caleb could do to lift it between them tied to a pole they had cut out of the brush.

All in all they explored the land for 40 days before meeting up with the other ten spies who'd been spying out the Desert of Zin as far as Rehob, toward Lebo Hamath. As they all headed back toward the Hebrew camp at Kadesh in the Desert of Paran, Joshua and Caleb's enthusiasm was soon dampened by the depressed and crushed spirits of their comrades. All they could do was complain in despair.

"Did you see the size of those city walls?"

"Yeah, they're impenetrable!"

"Not to mention how huge those soldiers were."

"I know, I saw one at least nine feet tall and built like an ox."

"I felt like a little grasshopper bouncing around a man's feet hoping he won't notice me and crush me underfoot!"

"Seriously, there's no way we can take this land…"

"Yep, once again, good ol' Moses has led us to a dead end."

"I knew it was too good to be true."

Whenever Caleb and Joshua tried to say anything positive about how rich the land was or how beautiful or how promising, they were mocked into silence by the others. Finally, they decided to just keep their mouths shut and wait till they got back to camp. They couldn't believe how quickly the others had forgotten all the miracles that had led them out of slavery and across the Red Sea. How could they have so quickly forgotten the awesome presence of Jehovah on the mountain?

Finally, tired, filthy and exhausted physically and emotionally, the 12 spies arrived back at Kadesh. After washing up and having some manna, they were called to present their findings to Moses and the Counsel.

"Okay, okay everyone, quiet down," said Moses, hands raised as he called the session to order. "When I sent you all out, I asked you to see what the land is like and whether the people who live there are strong or weak, few or many. I wanted to find out what kind of land they live in. Is it good or bad? What kind of towns do they live in? Are they unwalled or fortified? How is the soil? Is it fertile or poor? Are there trees on it or not? Now, you have been gone for 40 days and I am anxious to hear your reports."

There was a moment of silence as the 12 spies looked at each other. Finally, Shammua from the tribe of Reuben spoke up, pointing at the cluster of grapes Caleb and Joshua had set to the side of the entrance to the tent.

"We went into the land to which you sent us, and it does flow with milk and honey! Here is its fruit."

"But the people who live there are powerful," Palti of Benjamin interrupted. "And the cities are fortified and very large. We even saw descendants of Anak there."

"The Amalekites live in the Negev," interjected Sethur from the clan of Asher. "The Hittites, Jebusites and Amorites live in the hill country, and the Canaanites live near the sea and along the Jordan."

Then Caleb raised his hand, waited for things to quiet down and then said, "We should go up and take possession of the land, for we can certainly do it."

But those who had gone up with him retorted, "We can't attack those people. They're stronger than we are."

Th e argu men t went b ck and forth with Caleb and Josh u a encouraging the others to not be afraid and put their trust in Jehovah and the other ten telling Moses that it was impossible. Moses finally adjourned for the day without coming to any conclusion.

All that day and night, rumors buzzed around the camp. While Caleb and Joshua slept, the other returned spies went out among the people, spreading a bad report about the land they had scouted out.

"The land we explored devours those living in it."

"All the people we saw there are of great size."

"We saw the Nephilim there, the descendants of Anak the Giant."

"We seemed like grasshoppers in our own eyes, and we looked the same to them."

"'The people are stronger and taller than we are!'"

"The cities are large, with walls up to the sky!"

That night all the people of the community cried and wept. All the Israelites grumbled against Moses and Aaron, and the whole assembly gathered in front of their tent.

"If only we had died in Egypt!"

"Or in this desert!"

"Why is Jehovah bringing us to this land only to let us be killed?"

"Our wives and children will be taken as plunder."

"Wouldn't it be better for us to go back to Egypt?"

"Jehovah hates us. He brought us out of Egypt to destroy us!"

"Where can we go?"

"We should choose a different leader!"

"Let's go back to Egypt."

Then Moses and Aaron fell face down in front of the whole Israelite assembly gathered there. Joshua and Caleb tore their clothes and spoke to the entire group.

"The land we passed through and explored is amazingly good," said Joshua.

"If Jehovah is with us," added Caleb. "He will lead us into that rich land and will give it to us."

"Only don't rebel against Jehovah!" pleaded Joshua.

"And don't be afraid of those giants," continued Caleb. "We will swallow them up. Their protection is gone, but Jehovah is with us. Don't be afraid of them."

"Do not be terrified...do not be afraid of them," Joshua begged. "Jehovah, our God, will lead the way."

"Jehovah will fight for us," added Caleb. "As he did for us in Egypt and in the desert. There you saw how Jehovah carried us, as a father carries his son, all the way until we reached this place."

But as Joshua and Caleb pleaded with them, the crowd started to pick up rocks and talked about stoning them.

Just at that moment, the presence of Jehovah appeared at the Tent of Meeting in a blaze of glory. Out of the fire and smoke, Jehovah spoke to Moses.

"How long will these people treat me with contempt? How long will they refuse to believe in me, in spite of all the miraculous signs I have performed for them? I will strike them down with a plague and destroy them, but I will make you into a nation greater and stronger than they."

As the people fell on their faces in terror, Moses interceded with Jehovah.

"By your power you brought these people up from among the Egyptians. The inhabitants of this land have heard that you, the God of Abraham, are with these people. They know that you have been seen face to face, that your cloud stays over the Hebrews, and that you go before them in a pillar of cloud by day and a pillar of fire by night. If you put these people to death all at one time, these nations will say that you weren't able to do all that you promised in bringing the Israelites into this land.

"Now, let Jehovah's strength be displayed. In accordance with your great love, forgive the sin of these people, just as you have pardoned them from the time they left Egypt until now."

"I have forgiven them, as you asked," Jehovah replied. "Nevertheless, as surely as I live not one of the men who saw my glory and the miraculous signs I performed in Egypt and in the desert will ever see the land I promised to their forefathers. No one who has treated me with contempt will ever see it. But because Caleb has a different spirit and follows me wholeheartedly, I will bring him into the land he went to, and his descendants will inherit it."

Moses came out from meeting with Jehovah and addressed the people who were still prostrate in the dust. "Jehovah has told me to tell you: in this desert your bodies will fall, just as you feared, every one of you 20 years old or more who has grumbled against me. Not one of you will enter the promised land, except Caleb son of Jephunneh the Kenizzite and Joshua son of Nun.

"Your children will be shepherds here for forty years, suffering for your unfaithfulness, until the last of your bodies lies in the desert. For 40 years—one year for each of the 40 days you explored the land—you will suffer for your rebellion."

Immediately, the men who had been sent out by Moses to spy out the land fell down dead in front of the people. Of the men who went to explore the land, only Joshua and Caleb survived.

As Caleb leans on his spear, reflecting on the past and the painful 40 years of wandering in the desert, his men finally catch up with him on the brow of the hill. They are a motley crew, men from the tribe of Judah as well as the descendants of Moses' father-in-law, Jethro the Kenite, who had come up to join Caleb from Jericho.

So, here he is, 45 years later, about to do what he has waited almost half a century to do. He's on his way to take Kiriath Arba and the Valley of Eschol. Sure, the giants are still there, but he believed Jehovah would help him those many long years ago and since then he has seen Jehovah do even more. He's walked on dry ground across the Jordan River. He's watched the walls of Jericho fall. Jehovah is the Great God and he made Caleb a promise a long time ago. Now Caleb fully expects Jehovah to keep his end of the bargain.

With a triumphant gleam in his eyes, Caleb faces his men. "Alright, today's the day! If Jehovah is for us, who can be against us? Who's with me? WHO is WITH me? WHHHOOO?"

Yelling and shouting, an 85-year-old warrior at their lead, the Calebites storm exuberantly down the hill and never look back until Kiriath Arba becomes Caleb's, who renames it Hebron. From there, they advance against the people living in Kiriath Sepher and the rest of the cities of southern Canaan. As they settle in to their new country, the Calebites came to be known as the people of the desert of Judah (the Negev of Caleb) where they live in close relation to the traders from nearby Arabia, their brothers, the Children of the East.

Soon after the death of Caleb and Joshua, the children of Israel start what becomes a bad habit for them. They drift away from the one true God until they are abandoned into the hands of their enemies. Then they repent and cry out to Jehovah. Jehovah hears them and sends them a prophet or a judge to deliver them. Things go well until that prophet or judge dies. Then the process repeats itself.

One day the Israelites find themselves once again enslaved by their enemies. They repent of their idol worship and come to a prophetess named Deborah to ask for Jehovah's help. She calls upon a man named Barak to deliver Israel. He agrees, but only if she accompanies him. As a result, Deborah predicts that the glory for the victory will belong to a woman.

No one suspects it will be a quiet woman from the Children of the East...

Jael & Deborah

Most blessed of women be Jael,
The wife of Heber the Kenite,
Most blessed of tent-dwelling women.

Judges 5:24 (NIV)

There is no compulsion in religion:
True direction is already distinct from error...
God is the protector of believers,
Taking them out of the darkness
Into the light.

Qur'an 2:256-257

Jael sits under the great tree of Zaanannim and stares out over the rolling hills toward Kedesh. As a flock of ravens flies by overhead across the deep blue sky she wonders how the battle's going. For 20 years she and her husband, Heber the Kenite, have been on friendly terms with the Canaanites from Hazor. This was a smart business move on her husband's part and has brought them no little prosperity while the surrounding Israelites from Naphtali have become virtual slaves.

Jael is devoted to her husband and usually submits to him, as a good woman should. But she also has a stubborn, independent side. She never questioned Heber's decision to align himself with the kingdom of Jabin, at least not until today. As she sits under the ancient tree of the Kenites feeling the cool breeze of early evening wash across her face, for some reason, she thinks back to the stories her father used to tell her as she sat on his knee around the family fire.

"Ah, yes, my little Jael. You must never forget that you descend from greatness and Jehovah has great things in mind for you my little butterfly. My grandfather, and your great-grandpa, was none other than the mighty Hobab, the son of Reuel, the high priest of Midian and Moses' father-in-law. Yes, Moses married Hobab's sister, Zipporah, and had two sons by her before returning to Egypt to liberate the Children of Isaac from slavery.

"When Jethro Reuel met Moses again at Mount Sinai to bring him back his wife and sons, Hobab accompanied them. When Jethro left to return to his people in the East, Hobab wanted to go back, too. But Moses insisted that he stay. Without Hobab's expertise in those desert lands, the children of Isaac would've been lost for sure.

"Along with Caleb, son of Jephunneh the Kenizzite, Hobab and the rest of our ancestors, the Kenites, joined the tribe of Judah. Most of them settled to the south in the Negev, but our family came up here near the tribe of Naphtali, where we settled by this vintage tree of Zaanannim. We have been here ever since.

"So don't forget, little one, that we go back to the son of the great Jethro who taught Moses the truth about our God, Jehovah. Jethro received this knowledge directly from Ishmael and Midian, Abraham's sons. We've always been brothers with these Israelites, these sons of Isaac. Don't let people tell you we're different just because we live in tents and don't plant crops. We worship the same God and it's he who unites us."

A flash of lightening and the clash of pealing thunder brings Jael rudely back to the present. Looking across the plain to Mount Tabor, she sees the summit engulfed in rain and covered with angry clouds. She wonders silently how this will affect the battle being fought on the mountain slopes and down in the valley below. The area is prone to flash floods ripping through the wadis and would be to the advantage of the tribes fighting with Barak and Deborah against Jabin and Sisera.

Just a few months ago, when Jael went to Kedesh for market day, she heard rumors of the Prophetess Deborah. Apparently, Jehovah had revealed to her that because of the change of heart of the Israelites, he was ready to deliver them from the cruel oppression of Jabin and the Canaanites. Deborah was well known throughout Israel for her wisdom and ability to settle disputes. She held court under a palm tree between Ramah and Bethel in the hill country of Ephraim and people came from all over to seek her advice.

After getting the message from Jehovah about his desire to deliver Israel, she had sent to Kedesh for one of Naphtali's own: Barak son of Abinoam. Abinoam's son was not known for his bravery. In fact, he was a thin, shy man who mostly kept to himself. But who was he to refuse a call from Israel's most famous woman?

So Barak went to the Palm of Deborah. When he heard that he was supposed to lead the rebellion against Jabin, he panicked. Only with Deborah's agreement to go out to battle with him did Barak finally accept the challenge. Since then, the two of them had been quietly amassing an army of 10,000 men.

Finally, just a few days ago, the army of Barak and Deborah came out into the open and moved toward Mount Tabor. Yesterday, Sisera, King Jabin's commander-in-chief arrived from Hazor with their 900 chariots.

Since the morning, even from this distance, Jael can hear the awful sounds of war as the clashing of iron and the screams of the wounded drifts across the plains.

Whose side am I on? Jael is torn. She hasn't really thought about it much. She just went along with her husband's alliance with Hazor. But with the visions of her father's stories drifting back into her consciousness, she now feels that maybe she is on the wrong side. Haven't her ancestors, the Children of the East, those other children of Abraham, always been called on by Jehovah to help their brothers when the line of Isaac found itself in trouble?

As Jael looks down at the fierce antelope with the huge, curved horns embroidered on her robe, she finds herself carried back again in time. This time, she is on her mother's lap as she spins some rough wool into yarn.

"Yes, my little daughter. Do you know what your name means? Jael is the Hebrew name for a great and powerful animal: the Nubian ibex. When I looked down at you, my first born, I prayed to Jehovah that he would give you strength to fulfill his purpose for your life. That same night, your father came back from hunting telling about his unsuccessful attempt to bring down a powerful male ibex with massive horns. As I marveled at the majesty of that creature, I knew Jehovah wanted me to name you after her. You will be strong when facing your enemies for Jehovah himself will be with you in your darkest moment.

In my darkest moment... Once again, Jael is jolted out of her reverie. This time, it's by a movement on the plain below. A man on a horse is galloping furiously along, keeping to the brush as if fleeing from mortal danger. Jael watches fascinated, all thoughts for personal safety somehow washed from her mind. Slowly and then faster and faster the distance closes between Jael and the rider.

Soon, Jael recognizes the man as none other than Sisera himself, the Hazorite general! At first, her heart leaps in excitement at receiving so important a guest. But it is soon replaced by panic as she realizes he must be fleeing a losing battle. Have Barak and the Israelites really won after all? Did Jehovah come to their rescue?

Jael doesn't have much more time to think. She stands up just in time to bow in courtesy as Sisera bounds from the saddle and swats his horse's rump sending him galloping off in a cloud of dust.

"Good woman, I hear good things of your husband, Heber, our friend and ally. Can I impose on your hospitality, I am tired and hungry from a long day of riding."

While seeming to trust her, Sisera obviously isn't going to tell her the whole truth. But in her heart, Jael knows and her mind is made up about what to do.

"Oh great one, your legend proceeds you. It would be my honor to have the mighty Sisera be my guest. My husband is away, but come into his tent where you can refresh yourself. Don't be afraid."

Sisera goes into the tent and collapses onto a pile of cushions in the corner.

"I'm thirsty, please give me some water."

Going out to her own tent, Jael's mind races. *How can I do what I feel I'm supposed to do? Am I really the strong ibex my mother named me for? Will I really be able to come to the aid of my brothers like my father advised?*

A plan already formulating in her mind, Jael grabs a skin filled with sour camel's milk and goes back in to Sisera. Sisera drinks thankfully from the pouch and then leans back on the rich carpets covering the floor as he wipes the rest of the milk from his mustache.

"Woman, stand in the doorway of the tent. If anyone comes by and asks if anyone is here, tell him 'No!'" With that, Sisera falls into a deep slumber.

Gently closing the flap of the tent, Jael works quickly and silently. Behind the sheep pen she finds the things she's looking for and furtively conceals them in the folds of her garment. Then she tip-toes back to the tent where Sisera lies sleeping peacefully.

Careful not to make any sound, Jael inches her way across the rugs until she is poised over Sisera's gently snoring form. She lowers herself silently to the ground at the general's head. Taking out a metal tent stake she places its tip over Sisera's pulsating temple. Raising the large mallet with her other hand she swings down with all her strength…

Later that week, as the people celebrate their victory and freedom in Kedesh, Jael sits off to one side deep in thought. Gently over the night air a haunting song comes wafting over the slowly sleeping town. It is the voice

of Deborah singing what would become one of Israel's most beloved
songs:

Because the leaders took the lead in Israel
Because the people offered themselves willingly
Be blessed, Jehovah!
Hear, you kings!
Give ear, you princes!
I, even I, will sing to Jehovah
I will sing praise to Jehovah, the God of Israel

Jehovah, when you went forth out of Seir
When you marched out of the field of Edom
The earth trembled, the sky also dropped
Yes, the clouds dropped water
The mountains quaked
At the presence of Jehovah

In the days of Jael, the highways were unoccupied
The travelers walked through byways
The rulers ceased in Israel
They ceased until I, Deborah, arose
Until I arose a mother in Israel

Then the people of Jehovah went down to the gates.
Awake, awake, Deborah!
Awake, awake, utter a song!
Arise, Barak, and lead away your captives
Then a remnant of the nobles and the people came down
Jehovah came down for me against the mighty

The kings came and fought
They took no plunder of silver
From the sky the stars fought
From their courses, they fought against Sisera
The river Kishon swept them away
My soul, march on with strength

Jael shall be blessed above women
The wife of Heber the Kenite
Blessed shall she be above women in the tent
He asked for water

She gave him milk
She brought him butter in a lordly dish

She put her hand to the tent peg
Her right hand to the workmen's hammer
With the hammer she struck Sisera
She struck through his head
Yes, she pierced and struck through his temples

At her feet he bowed, he fell, he lay
At her feet he bowed, he fell
Where he bowed, there he fell down dead
So let all your enemies perish, Jehovah
But let those who love him be as the sun
When it rises forth in its strength

Israel lived through many more judges and prophets until one day they asked for a king. The prophet Samuel grudgingly ceded to their request and anointed Saul as the first King of Israel. Saul soon began following his own ways so after his death there was a civil war between Saul's son Ish-Bosheth and David. A man named Rechab, along with a friend, murdered Ish-Bosheth and was summarily executed by David.

Rechab's son, Jonadab, chose a different path, retreating to the desert until he was called by Jehovah to meet up with an old friend named Jehu...

Jehu & Jonadab

He came upon Jonadab son of Rechab,
Who was on his way to meet him.
Jehu greeted him and said,
"Are you in accord with me, as I am with you?"
"I am," Jonadab answered.
"If so," said Jehu, "give me your hand."
So he did, and Jehu helped him up into the chariot.
Jehu said, "Come with me and see my zeal for [Jehovah]."
Then he had him ride along in his chariot.

2 Kings 10:15-16 (NIV)

As for those who believed,
And those who went into exile
And struggled in the cause of God,
They look forward to the mercy of God;
And God is most forgiving,
Most merciful.

Qur'an 2:218

Jonadab is standing in Jehu's chariot just behind King Ahab's when he sees Elijah for the first time. He has heard many stories about the prophet, but this is the first time he's actually seen him. He remembers his uncles sitting around talking about the great miracle on Mount Carmel. Apparently, Elijah had challenged King Ahab to a sort of duel between Ahab's god, Baal, and Elijah's God, Jehovah. They had been on the mountain when it happened.

All day long the 400 priests of Baal had jumped around, chanting and dancing and cutting themselves trying to get their god to send down fire as proof of his power. Finally, Elijah's turn came just as the sun was setting. As he prayed to Jehovah, fire came down from a cloudless sky and burned up the offering and the stones of the altar, despite all of it having been soaked in barrels of water.

All of the priests of Baal were killed and it seemed like the nation would return to worshipping Jehovah, until the next morning when Queen Jezebel heard about it. She sent word immediately to Elijah that she was going to kill him. Uncharacteristically, Elijah tucked his tail between his legs and ran. No one knew exactly what happened to Elijah, but he disappeared into the wilderness for several months before coming back looking even wilder than usual.

Since his return from the desert, Elijah had kept a pretty low profile. He wandered through some of the smaller villages, mostly in the company of a young man named Elisha, who had become Elijah's apprentice. So, when Elijah shows up today, everyone is shocked to see him. Ahab had just taken Jehu and a few of his army officers out to his newly acquired vineyard. No one expected to encounter a fire-breathing prophet.

"So, you have found me, my enemy?" sneers Ahab, addressing Elijah. As the two long-time rivals face each other, Jehu moves his chariot around from behind Ahab's to get a closer look at the infamous prophet.

As a seasoned warrior and commander of Ahab's army, the first thing Jehu notices is Elijah's physical presence. Although of average height and weight, years of hardship and rustic living have made the prophet lean and tough. His long, matted beard and hair stick out in all directions. Leathery, wrinkled skin from long hours under the unforgiving Palestinian sun poke out from under a rough robe of camel skin tied carelessly around his waist with a belt of camel hair. His bare feet hug the earth fiercely like a man used to standing his ground. His piercing eyes bore into Ahab as he pronounces his judgment from Jehovah.

"I've found you," Elijah answers, "because you have sold yourself to do evil in the eyes of Jehovah. I heard how you and Jezebel had Naboth murdered so you could steal his vineyard. Wasn't it enough that Jehovah permitted you to be king of his people? You have let yourself be consumed with your own selfishness and greed. Now listen to Jehovah's judgment upon you:

"'I am going to bring disaster on you. I will consume your descendants. You have provoked me and have caused Israel to sin.'

"And as for your wife, Jezebel," Elijah continues. "Jehovah says: 'Dogs will devour Jezebel by the wall of Jezreel. Dogs will eat those belonging to Ahab who die in the city, and the birds of the air will feed on those who die in the country.'"

Jonadab watches fascinated and paralyzed. Normally, if someone dared to speak to the king like that, Jehu would have arrested him immediately. But something more powerful than any human power he has known keeps Jehu standing stunned and immobile in his chariot as he watches Elijah casually walk away through the vineyard. Ahab's response is even more remarkable.

Ahab watches Elijah until he disappears. Then the king grabs the front of his expensive robe and rips it right down the middle leaving him naked except for his loincloth. Ahab then tears at his head and beard, slapping his head wildly as he wails like a sorrowing woman. He then jumps out of his chariot onto the ground and begins tossing dust up in the air until he's covered from head to toe.

Jonadab almost feels sorry for Ahab. While he has never really respected the man, he does have to admit that he himself might not have acted much differently if he'd had the poor luck to be married to a woman like Jezebel. She is a fierce, cunning and cruel psychopath who always seems to know just how to get her way. The curious thing is that, despite the evil always lurking just under the surface, she can be one of the most charming people he's ever met. She uses her stunning beauty as a tool for manipulating and controlling lesser beings. Jonadab is always on his guard in her presence as he feels that he too could somehow come under her spell if he's not careful.

As the king's party returns somberly home, Jehu and Jonadab discuss the prophet and his message from Jehovah. They have both secretly been believers in Jehovah since childhood.

"Jonadab, my friend," Jehu starts out. "I've been struggling with this whole Jehovah thing recently. Do you think he's abandoned us?"

"I don't know, maybe," Jonadab replies carefully. "Don't you think it's just that most of our brothers have abandoned him?"

"I guess," Jehu continues gingerly. "I just feel so often that I'm the only one—or I guess WE are the only ones—who even remember Jehovah at all."

"Yeah, for a while, after Mount Carmel, I thought things would change, but they didn't. Even Elijah fled."

"But now he's back. Don't you think this could be the start of something? I mean, I've always felt like Jehovah had some plan for my life, something big for me to do…"

"I know what you mean, like we're a part of something much bigger, and we have an important role to play…I've always thought that too."

They continue back to Samaria in silence, each lost in his own thoughts. Little does Jehu know at the time, that this is the last time he will see Jonadab for 15 years.

Many years pass without incident for Jehu. Ahab is killed in battle and succeeded by his son, Ahaziah who reigns for two years before dying of injuries sustained in a fall. Since Ahaziah has no sons, his brother Joram takes the throne.

Meanwhile, Jehu continues to work in the army, participates in a few battles, trains more soldiers, and does all the other things that warriors do. But, the feeling that Jehovah has a plan for his life is beginning to fade. It's tough when everyone around him worships Baal. In fact, Jehu finds it easier and easier to just go along with all the rest as they perform their meaningless rites and rituals in the big temple in Samaria. But Jehu's heart isn't in it.

For one thing, he keeps hearing stories, miraculous stories. He hears a wild tale of Elijah calling down fire from heaven to consume two groups of 50 soldiers before Elijah himself is taken up to heaven in chariots of fire. Elisha then literally picks up Elijah's cloak and parts the Jordan River with it so he can walk across on dry land.

The stories about Elisha, in fact, are even more amazing than Elijah's: purifying the water in Jericho with a bowel of salt; sending two bears to attack some youths who'd made fun of him; saving the armies of Israel and Judah in the desert by making water appear in dry ditches overnight without rain; helping a widow with a never-ending jar of oil that fills up a houseful of large pots; raising a dead boy to life; multiplying a few loaves of bread so they feed a hundred men; healing Aram's general, Naaman, of leprosy by bathing in the river; and making an ax head float.

Jehu himself is present one day in Samaria when Elisha shows up leading the entire Aramean army by the hand. Apparently, they had gone to try and capture Elisha. Every time King Ben-Hadad tried to set an ambush for the Israelites, Jehovah would tell Elisha exactly where they were so Israel could avoid them. So, when the Aramean army showed up outside the gates of Elisha's town, he simply prayed and Jehovah blinded every last one of the enemy soldiers! Elisha then proceeds to escort them straight to their enemy's capital city where he presents them to the king.

"Shall I kill them? Shall I kill them?" King Joram is ecstatic as he begs Elisha for the chance for revenge.

"No," Elisha answers. "Would you kill men you have captured with your own sword or bow? Set food and water before them so that they may eat and drink and then go back to their master."

Jehu immediately sees the wisdom in Elisha's counsel. No easterner could ever fight against someone with whom he has shared a meal. According to local custom, they have become brothers.

The Arameans eventually do come back, though, and Jehu survives the siege of Samaria that gets so desperate that some women even eat their own children. Finally, following one of Elijah's prophecies, Jehovah miraculously delivers them. The enemy army hears the sound of chariots and marching men in the night and flees. They thought the Israelites had made a pact with Egypt and the Hittites who were coming to the rescue.

But Jehu still feels like Jehovah isn't fulfilling the call he's felt on his life for so many years. In fact, now 15 years have gone by since that day in Naboth's vineyard when he'd come face to face with Elijah and felt the real presence of Jehovah. *Will Jehovah ever act?* Nothing seems to change.

Now, Jehu and the Israelite army is in yet another war with the Arameans. Their new king, Hazael, murdered Ben-Hadad, took the throne of Aram and soon mounted an attack on Israel. King Joram went to battle at Ramoth Gilead and was wounded. While the rest of the army continues the defense, Joram retreats to Jezreel where he can recover from his injuries.

Ahaziah, King of Judah, is King Joram's nephew so he goes to Jezreel to visit him in his convalescence. Meanwhile, Jehu is in Ramoth Gilead with the rest of the troops. One evening, as he's sitting outside the army barracks with some of the other officers, a disheveled young man walks purposefully into the courtyard.

"I am seeking Jehu, son of Jehoshaphat, son of Nimshi," the youth announces

He can't be more than 16, but he has an air of authority about him. His simple cloak is tucked into his belt and he's covered with the dust of a long journey. In his right hand he carries a flask with a piece of wood stuck in the top as a stopper.

"Yeah, that's me," Jehu casually replies as he looks up from the stick he's been whittling with his dagger. "Who are you and what do you want?"

"I come from Elisha," the boy fixes his steel grey eyes on Jehu. "I have a message for you, commander."

Jehu is a little taken aback. He straightens up and leans forward. "For which of us?" he demands, not sure what to make of this boy.

"For you, commander," he replies, looking again squarely in Jehu's eyes.

Jehu is intrigued. He stands up and motions for the messenger to follow him. They duck into the privacy of Jehu's house and once inside he turns to face the young prophet.

Pulling the cork out of his flask, the young man reaches up and begins solemnly pouring oil over Jehu's head. Jehu is too stunned to react. He just stares into the prophet's eyes as he speaks.

"This is what Jehovah, the God of Israel, says: 'I anoint you king over Jehovah's people Israel. You are to destroy the house of Ahab your master, and I will avenge the blood of my servants shed by Jezebel. The whole house of Ahab will perish. As for Jezebel, dogs will devour her on the plot of ground at Jezreel, and no one will bury her.'"

With that, the unnamed messenger turns and runs out the open door without looking back. Jehu stands a few moments inside, massaging the oil into his scalp. He calms his racing thoughts as he feels Jehovah's presence, as he's never felt it before. This is the time for him to become who he is meant to be. He steps outside and rejoins his companions.

"Is everything all right?" one of the officers looks up at Jehu, eyes questioning. "Why did this madman come to you?"

"You know that type of man and the sort of things he says," Jehu replies.

"No we don't!" the men say. "Tell us."

"Here's what he told me," Jehu responds. "'This is what Jehovah says: I anoint you king over Israel.'"

His men look stunned for a second and then let out a rousing cheer as they spread their cloaks on the steps under the newly anointed king.

"Jehu is King! Jehu is King! Jehu is King!"

"If this is the way you feel," Jehu says. "Don't let anyone slip out of the city or they'll go and tell the news in Jezreel."

All business, Jehu runs to his chariot, which is always kept on the ready and grabs the reins from the stable boy. He jumps in while barking out orders to his men on how to secure the city. Slapping the reins against the two horses' backs, Jehu takes the road to Jezreel as the rest of his charioteers try desperately to keep up with his mad pace.

As the tower in Jezreel comes into view, Jehu notices a cloud of dust leave the city gates and rapidly approach until it turns into a single rider on a lathered up horse who pulls up to Jehu's chariot just as Jehu reins in his own team.

"This is what the king says," gasps the man, struggling to regain his breath after the hard ride. "'Do you come in peace?'"

"What do you have to do with peace?" Jehu replies. "Fall in behind me."

Not knowing what else to do and faced with a group of very serious and determined men all staring at him, the young messenger maneuvers his horse around behind the chariots as they continue their race toward Jezreel.

Soon, another horseman pulls up asking the same question and getting the same answer from Jehu. Meanwhile, back in Jezreel, the lookout on the tower reports back to King Joram.

"The second messenger has reached them, but he isn't coming back either. The lead charioteer is driving like Jehu son of Nimshi—he drives like a madman."

"Hitch up my chariot," Joram orders.

When the chariots are ready, King Joram and King Ahaziah of Judah ride out together, each in his own chariot, to meet Jehu. They meet him at the plot of ground that had belonged to Naboth the Jezreelite.

Coming up to Jehu, Joram asks, "Have you come in peace, Jehu?"

"How can there be peace," Jehu replies. "As long as all the idolatry and witchcraft of your mother Jezebel is still around?"

Joram turns about and tries to flee, calling out, "Treachery, Ahaziah!"

Jehu draws his bow and shoots Joram between the shoulders. The arrow pierces his heart and he slumps down in his chariot.

Jehu turns to Bidkar, his chariot officer. "Remember how you and I were riding together in chariots behind Ahab his father when Elijah made this prophecy about him: *I saw the blood of Naboth and the blood of his sons, declares Jehovah, and I will surely make you pay for it on this plot of ground?*"

"Yes, of course," Bidkar replies. "It was right over there, in that vineyard."

"Now then," continues Jehu. "Pick him up and throw him on that plot, and fulfill Jehovah's prophecy!"

When Ahaziah king of Judah sees what's happened, he flees up the road to Beth Haggan with Jehu and his men in pursuit.

"Kill him too!" Jehu shouts.

They wound Ahaziah in his chariot on the way up to Gur near Ibleam, but he escapes to Megiddo and dies there. His servants take him by chariot to Jerusalem and bury him with his fathers in their tomb.

Meanwhile, Jehu continues on to Jezreel. When Jezebel hears about it, she puts on makeup, arranges her hair and waits by a window. As Jehu enters the gate, she calls out to him.

"Have you come in peace, Jehu son of Nimshi, you murderer of your master?"

Jehu looks up at the window and calls out, "Who's with me? Who?"

Two or three eunuchs look down at him.

"Throw her down!" Jehu cries.

So they grab her and throw her out the window to the ground. Her blood spatters the wall and the horses as they trample her underfoot.

Jehu goes in to the palace to eat and drink, celebrating his victory.

"Take care of that cursed woman," he says after awhile. "Bury her, for she was a king's daughter."

But when some of the soldiers go to bury her, they find nothing except her skull, her feet and her hands. They return and tell Jehu.

"This is the word of Jehovah that he spoke through his servant Elijah the prophet," Jehu responds. "'On the plot of ground at Jezreel dogs will devour Jezebel's flesh. Jezebel's body will be like refuse on the ground, so that no one will be able to say, "This is Jezebel.""'"

The next day, Jehu writes letters and sends them to Samaria to the city officials and elders.

"Since Ahab's sons are with you and you have chariots and horses, a fortified city and weapons," Jehu writes. "Choose the best and most worthy of the sons and set him on his father's throne. Then fight for your master's house."

As soon as they receive the letters, all of the leaders in Samaria get together to discuss what to do. They're terrified and say, "If two kings could not resist him, how can we?"

So the palace administrator, the city governor, the elders and the guardians send a message to Jehu: "We are your servants and we will do anything you say. We will not appoint anyone as king. Do whatever you think best."

Then Jehu writes them a second letter, saying, "If you are on my side and will obey me, take the heads of your master's sons and come to me in Jezreel by this time tomorrow."

Now the royal princes, 70 of them, were living with the leading men of the city, who were rearing them. When the letter arrives, these men take the princes and slaughter all 70 of them. They put their heads in baskets and send them to Jehu in Jezreel. When the messenger arrives with the heads, he goes immediately to see Jehu.

"Here they are," he says. "I've brought the heads of the princes as requested."

"Put them in two piles at the entrance of the city gate," Jehu orders. "Leave them there until morning."

The next morning Jehu goes out and stands before all the people and addresses them.

"You are innocent. It was I who conspired against my master and killed him, but who killed all these?" Jehu points to the piles of heads. "Know then, that not a word that Jehovah has spoken against the house of Ahab will fail. Jehovah has done what he promised through his servant Elijah."

Jehu then proceeds to kill everyone in Jezreel who is left of the house of Ahab, as well as all his chief men, his close friends and his priests, leaving him no survivor.

Jehu then sets out for Samaria. At Beth Eked of the Shepherds, he meets some relatives of King Ahaziah.

"Who are you?" he asks.

"We are relatives of Ahaziah," they reply. "We have come down to greet the families of the king and of the queen mother."

"Take them alive!" Jehu orders the soldiers with him.

So they take them alive and slaughter them by the well of Beth Eked —forty-two men, leaving no survivors.

After leaving Beth Eked, Jehu runs into Jonadab son of Rechab, who is on his way to meet him. Jehu greets him.

"Are you in accord with me, as I am with you?"

"I am," Jonadab answers.

"If so," says Jehu. "Give me your hand."

Jonadab reaches up and Jehu helps him up into the chariot.

"Come with me and see my zeal for Jehovah." Then Jehu and Jonadab take off together in Jehu's chariot. After riding in silence for a few miles, Jehu breaks the silence.

"Where have you been these last few years, my friend? It's been a long time."

"After that day in Naboth's vineyard, I felt Jehovah calling me to learn more of him. So I left my family and went to live with the prophets who were hiding from Jezebel. I finally heard the story of what happened to Elijah after Mount Carmel..."

"Really, I've always wondered at his disappearing act."

"I guess even someone as strong as Elijah has his weaknesses. After facing up to Ahab and the 400 prophets of Baal, Elijah fled as soon as Jezebel threatened him. If it hadn't been for the Angel of Jehovah giving him food and strengthening him in the desert he would have died. Elijah was then told by Jehovah to go to Mount Sinai, you know, the same mountain from all the old stories about Moses."

"Are you serious? I've sometimes wondered if all that wasn't just a myth."

"No, it really happened. Elijah was there and Jehovah spoke to him directly. And do you know what he said?"

"Of course, not, go on."

"He was told to appoint Elisha to replace him as prophet, which he did before disappearing in a chariot of fire right in front of Elisha."

"So the stories are true."

"Yeah, and all those stories about Elisha? They're true too. I was there for all of them. I even saw you from a distance in Samaria that day Elisha led in all the blind Arameans."

"Seriously? That was really impressive."

"But, the anointing of Elisha was not all that Jehovah told Elijah that day. Jehovah told him to anoint you king of Israel."

"What?!"

"Yes, that was several years before that time in Naboth's vineyard. Do you remember how you said you always felt Jehovah had something special in mind for you?"

"Yes, of course."

"Well, that was because Jehovah had already planned for what you are doing now a long time ago. I've been waiting for this moment for 15 years. So, when I heard that the revolution had started, I just had to find you!"

"Wow..." is all Jehu can say as they ride the rest of the way to Samaria in deep thought.

When they arrive in Samaria, Jehu kills all who are left there of Ahab's family. Afterwards, he gets together with Jonadab to strategize on how best to accomplish the religious reform that they feel Jehovah especially calling them to do. The main challenge is how pervasive the worship of Baal has become. How to get it all purged as quickly as possible? After many late nights, they finally hit upon the perfect plan.

The next day, Jehu gathers all the people together.

"Ahab served Baal a little; Jehu will serve him much," Jehu announces. "Now summon all the prophets of Baal, all his ministers and all his priests. See that no one is missing, because I am going to hold a great sacrifice for Baal. Anyone who fails to come will no longer live. Call an assembly in honor of Baal."

So the elders send word throughout Israel. All the ministers of Baal come. No one stays home. They crowd into the temple of Baal until it is full from one end to the other.

"Bring robes for all the ministers of Baal," Jehu tells the keeper of the wardrobe who brings out robes for each one.

Then Jehu and Jonadab son of Rechab enter the temple of Baal.

"Look around and see that no servants of Jehovah are here with you," orders Jehu. "Only ministers of Baal."

So the priests start to make sacrifices and burnt offerings. Meanwhile, Jehu posts eighty men outside the temple.

"If one of you lets any of the men I am placing in your hands escape," he warns. "It will be your life for his life."

As soon as Jehu finishes the burnt offering, he orders the guards and officers to go into the temple.

"Go in and kill them," he shouts. "Let no one escape!"

So the soldiers cut down the ministers of Baal with the sword. The guards and officers throw the bodies out and then enter the inner shrine. They bring the sacred stone out of the temple of Baal and burn it. They demolish everything inside and then tear down the entire temple. Ever since, the people now use the site for a latrine.

So Jehu destroys Baal worship in Israel. However, he continues to worship the golden calves at Bethel and Dan.

One day, Jonadab says to Jehu, "Listen to what Jehovah has told me concerning you and your zeal for him: 'Because you have done well in accomplishing what is right in my eyes and have done to the house of Ahab all I had in mind to do, your descendants will sit on the throne of Israel to the fourth generation.'"

After 28 years as king in Samaria, Jehu dies and is buried in Samaria. Meanwhile, Jonadab, always eager to take his spirituality to the next level, pursues a slightly different course. He moves to the desert and founds a group of ascetics, named after his father, called the Rechabites...

Rechabites

Therefore this is what the LORD Almighty
The God of Israel, says
"Jonadab son of Rechab will never fail
To have a descendant to serve me."

Jeremiah 35:19 (NIV)

Satan only wants to sow
Hostility and hatred among you
With wine and gambling,
And to hinder you
From remembrance of God,
And from prayer.
So will you refrain?

Qur'an 5:91

Jaazaniah moves briskly through the cobblestoned streets of Jerusalem. He's on his way to his family's house, but his mind is elsewhere. *What could Jeremiah possibly want with us at the Temple? Could this have something to do with our past? Will we never cease suffering for the sins of our fathers?* His thoughts drift back to that campfire years ago in the middle of the desert when his grandfather gathered the young boys around him to tell them a story.

"Boys, it's about time you heard our family story. It all started back in the days of King David when he was fighting Abner and Ish-Bosheth for the kingdom. King Saul had just been killed on the battlefield and his general, Abner, was trying to put his son, Ish-Bosheth, on the throne.

"Your great-great-great-great grandfather, Rechab, was a mighty warrior. He led a band of Kenite cavalry that had always been loyal to King Saul ever since the day Saul had saved them from certain death. Saul was going to go to war against the Amalekites, but sent word ahead of time to warn the Kenites to move away from them since our ancestors had helped the Israelites by guiding them through the desert after they escaped from Egypt. That's why our Kenite fathers, from the clan of Beeroth, moved away to Gittaim in the land of Benjamin.

"So, Rechab was loyal to Saul, of course, and fought alongside Abner against David. One day, however, Rechab and his cousin, Baanah, were sitting together having some wine. They drank too much and stopped thinking clearly. Rechab started talking about the futility of the war. It was obvious that David was going to win. They worried that David would kill them for having been loyal to Ish-Bosheth. That's when Baanah suggested something that neither would have considered if he hadn't been drunk.

"'Let's assassinate Ish-Bosheth...if we prove that we killed David's enemy, then that should save our lives,' said Baanah.

"So Rechab and Baanah got up from the table, set their wine cups down, wiped their red-stained mouths and beards, and marched off to the palace. They were well-known to the palace guards and got in with the simple lie that they were coming to get some wheat for their troops.

"It was the hottest part of the day and Ish-Bosheth had retired to his room to take a nap. Rechab and Banaah slipped in, stabbed him to death in the stomach and cut off his head. Wrapping the head in cloth, they emptied part of a sack of wheat, stuffed the head in, and walked out without anyone the wiser.

"Jumping on their horses they raced out of town toward David's camp. Arriving on the outskirts they gave themselves up and said they had a message for King David. Walking up to where David was sitting, listening to his advisors they triumphantly unwrapped Ish-Bosheth's head and dumped it ceremoniously at David's feet.

"All the advisors jumped to their feet in surprise. They then gathered around and soon recognized the head as Ish-Bosheth's. Not sure how to react they stepped back and waited as Rechab and Banaah explained what they'd done.

"'Behold, the head of Ish-Bosheth, the son of Saul, your enemy, who sought your life! Jehovah has avenged my lord the king this day of Saul, and of his seed.'

"David stood there stunned for a few minutes as everyone held their breath. Then David turned to Rechab and Banaah. The narrowed, tear-filled eyes of the King caused them to take a few steps back as he spoke:

"'As Jehovah lives, who has redeemed my soul out of all adversity, when someone told me, *Behold, Saul is dead,* thinking to have brought good news, I took hold of him, and killed him in Ziklag, which was the reward I gave him for his news. How much more, when wicked men have slain a righteous person in his own house on his bed, shall I not now require his blood of your hand, and take you away from the earth?!'

"Realizing their danger, Rechab and Banaah tried to flee but were easily overtaken and brought to the outskirts of camp where David's soldiers killed them. They cut off their hands and feet and hung them by the pool in Hebron."

Jaazaniah quickly suppresses the memory of his two relatives' mutilated bodies as he turns down a side alley to take a short cut home. Considering the shame brought on the Rechabite clan by their father's inglorious death, it was no wonder that Rechab's son, Jonadab, had forbidden his sons to drink wine. They had seen what could happen when under the influence of a substance that made you do things you would regret later.

As to why Jonadab had also told his descendants to never live in houses, sow seed or plant vineyards, Jaazaniah could also see the reasons for that from Jonadab's personal religious experience. It was out in the desert, free from the influences of city life, that Jonadab had come to know the one true God. After being called by Jehovah to help Jehu purify the land of the worship of Baal, Jonadab had seen how Jehu had been influenced by wealth and power. Jonadab had then retreated back into the simple life of the nomad to keep his family in touch with nature and its Creator.

Arriving at home, Jaazaniah quickly assembles the elders of the family and tells them about Jeremiah's invitation to join him in the Temple. They all respect Jeremiah and his courage in speaking Jehovah's unpopular messages to the people. They feel that a personal invitation by the prophet is an honor they can't refuse.

Walking together through the streets, they create quite an impression. Even though they are now living in the city, the Rechabites have lost none of the wildness of their Bedouin ways and the other pedestrians give them a wide birth. Arriving at the temple, the doorkeeper, Shallum, seems to be expecting them and lets them in without question, pointing them in the direction of an inner room.

As they enter the house of Jehovah, they see the prophet run out to meet them. His face is lined and wrinkled and his hair dark and long. A huge smile reveals crooked, yellowing teeth and his eyes twinkle. He opens his arms and embraces each of them with a warm, powerful hug.

"Peace be upon you! Come in, come in, I've been expecting you. Right this way." Jeremiah leads them down a passageway to the room of the sons of Hanan, son of Igdaliah, a prophet of Jehovah.

As Jaazaniah enters the bare room through the low doorway, his eye is drawn to the rough-hewn table in the center. Wooden cups are arranged haphazardly around the edges. In the center sit three bowls of sparkling, purple wine.

"Welcome, welcome," continues Jeremiah disarmingly. "Before we get started on the reason I've brought you here, refresh yourselves. Have some wine." And the prophet motions to the cups and bowls before them. The other Rechabites hesitate, looking to Jaazaniah for a sign.

Without hesitation, Jaazaniah looks Jeremiah square in the face and replies. "We don't drink wine. Our ancestor, Jonadab son of Rechab told us to never drink alcohol, build houses, or grow our own food. He told us that we were to be nomads, always living in tents if we wanted to live long lives.

"So, Jeremiah, we have always obeyed everything that Jonadab told us. Neither we nor our wives nor our sons nor our daughters have ever drunk wine, or built houses, or had vineyards, fields or crops. We live in tents and raise livestock and live as nomads.

"However, when the Babylonians invaded our land, we were forced to escape to Jerusalem and that's why we live here currently. But we still refuse to drink wine. Sorry to offend you as host, but I hope you understand."

With a small smile playing at his lips, Jeremiah slowly shakes his head in amazement as he looks upward with his hands outstretched.

"This is what Jehovah says to the people of Judah: 'Will you not receive instruction to listen to my words? The words of Jonadab the son of Rechab, that he commanded his sons, not to drink wine, are performed. To this day they drink none, for they obey their father's commandment. But I have spoken to you and you have not listened to me.

"'I have sent also to you all my servants the prophets, saying, "Return now every man from his evil way, and amend your doings. Don't go after other gods to serve them, and you shall dwell in the land which I have given to you and to your fathers." But you have not inclined your ear, nor listened to me.

"'The sons of Jonadab the son of Rechab have performed the commandment of their father which he commanded them, but this people has not listened to me. Therefore, I will bring on Judah and on all the inhabitants of Jerusalem all the evil that I have pronounced against them. I have spoken to them, but they have not heard. I have called to them, but they have not answered.'

"Thus says Jehovah, the God of Israel," Jeremiah then said to Jaazaniah and the other Rechabites. "You have obeyed the commandment of Jonadab your father, kept all his precepts, and done according to all that he commanded you. Therefore thus says Jehovah, the God of Israel: 'Jonadab the son of Rechab shall not want a man to stand before me forever.'"

Several decades later, in 586 BC, Nebuchadnezzar, king of Babylon, captures Jerusalem, tears down the city wall, and sets fire to the palace and other houses. The Babylonians kill all the Jewish officials, blind the king and take the educated Israelites to Babylon. They leave only the poor to continue cultivating the land. Nebuchadnezzar left Gedaliah the son of Ahikam as governor.

Nebuchadnezzar then sends a special message to the captain of the imperial guard, Nebuzaradan, concerning Jeremiah: "Take him, and look well to him, and do him no harm. But do whatever he asks."

So Nebuzaradan sends some men to rescue Jeremiah. When Jeremiah is brought before him, Nebuzaradan tells him, "Jehovah your God pronounced this evil on this place. He has done according as he spoke. Because you have sinned against Jehovah, and have not obeyed his voice, therefore this thing has come on you.

"Now, behold, I release you this day from your chains. If it seems good to you to come with me into Babylon, come, and I will take care of you. But if it seems bad to you to come with me into Babylon, don't. Behold, all the land is before you. Go back then to Gedaliah, whom the king of Babylon has made governor over the cities of Judah, and dwell with him among the people. Or go wherever it seems right to you to go."

Then the captain of the guard gives Jeremiah food and a present, and lets him go. Jeremiah decides to stay in Judah with Gedaliah. Jaazaniah and the Rechabites also are left in the land. When Gedaliah is assassinated and chaos breaks out in Judah, Jaazaniah leads the Rechabites back into the desert to the land of the Edomites.

The Babylonian captivity leaves a power vacuum in Judah. The Edomites, descendants of Esau and part of the Children of the East, move from their stronghold of Sela (Petra) near Mount Seir into the vacant Judean grazing lands. It's at this time that Nabataean inscriptions first begin to be left in Edomite territory.

The word *Nabataean* is Arabic for *Aramaen*. History tells us they were Arabs, as evidenced by their names, but their language was Aramaic. So when the Rechabites move into Edomite lands they begin to be called the Nabataeans because they are Aramaic-speaking Arabs.

In about 300 BC, the Nabataeans (Rechabites) capture the ancient Edomite stronghold of Mount Seir and their capital, Sela (or Petra as it came to be known in Greek) since many of the Edomites have abandoned their desert fortress for the newly-vacated Judean grazing lands.

As the world enters the Common Era, however, the Nabataeans' language comes more and more under the influence of Arabic. Eventually, the transformation from Aramaic to Arabic is complete.

From 8 BC to 40 AD, the King of Petra is a Nabataean named Aretas IV. During his reign, a child born to humble parents in Bethlehem is about to receive an unlikely visit from some of the Children of the East...

Wise Men

Now when Jesus was born...
Behold, wise men from the east came...saying
"Where is he who is born King of the Jews?
For we saw his star in the east
And have come to worship him."

Matthew 2:1-2

And mention Mary in the Book:
When she withdrew from her people
To a place in the East...
We sent her Our spirit...
He said, "I am only
A messenger from your Lord,
to give you a sinless son..."
That was Jesus, Son of Mary,
A word of truth about which they doubt.

Qur'an 19:16-19,34

Malik gazes up at the blazing sun. He is lying on his back on a sheepskin rug, hugging the side of his camel in a desperate attempt to elude the scorching heat of the desert. He has to admit, traveling at night does have its advantages. The camels tire less easily and need less water and food. The men accompanying Malik also are able to go faster and cover more ground. However, traveling at night means that one has to sleep during the day, or at least attempt to sleep despite the heat.

Malik swats a fly and rolls over onto his side. He's so tired after weeks in the saddle that in spite of the uncomfortable conditions, he is soon in dreamland.

He finds himself alone on top of a mountain gazing out across a fertile valley filled with tents. In the next instant, he is surrounded by figures that look like men, but have the faces of wolves. Malik looks around anxiously into hundreds of gleaming eyes and sharp toothed grins, tongues lolling and dripping saliva as if in anticipation of a bloody feast. Suddenly a cloaked figure comes hurtling toward him on a black donkey as a deep voice surges from the faceless creature, "Follow the star...follow the star...follow the star..."

Jolting upright, Malik wipes the sweat from his brow as he regains consciousness. Reaching for his water skin, he tries to calm his nerves. "Follow the star." Well that makes sense. That's what he's doing. As he slakes his thirst, Malik thinks back on the strange happenings of the last few months.

Coming from a family of priests, Malik had always been interested in philosophy and history, especially the history of his people's religion. Growing up on the banks of the Euphrates, he always felt comforted by the history that surrounded him. The weight of years of learning and power were still evident in the ruins of the great empires that could still be seen in many parts of the country: Assyria, Babylon, Media, Persia, Greece. All had left their mark.

What really interested him, though, was the study of astronomy. As a boy he always loved going outside at night and staring at the stars, wondering what, if anything, was up there beyond. His father told him how since the time of the ancient prophet, Balaam, his people had always looked to the stars. One of the earliest things that Malik learned to read was the ancient prophecies of Balaam that had been carefully preserved down through the ages. He especially loved the mysterious one that talked about a special, new star that would arise in the future signaling some important, metaphysical event:

Balaam the son of Beor says
Who hears the words of Jehovah
Knows the knowledge of the Most High
Who sees the vision of the Almighty
Falling down, and having his eyes open
"I see him, but not now
I see him, but not near
A star will come out of Jacob
A scepter will rise out of Israel"

Numbers 24:15-17

As he grew older, his father introduced Malik to some of the other prophecies that were in their possession: Zoroaster, Daniel, Isaiah, Jeremiah, all of which were readily available in the great libraries of Damascus. Malik was especially interested in the writings of Daniel, a Hebrew captive who became the prime minister of the Babylonian Empire and later on Media-Persian Empire. He was not only a political figure, but a prophet of Jehovah, the God worshipped by Malik and his family since the time of Abraham.

Malik discovered in one of the scrolls of Daniel another prophecy, which seemed to shed light on the importance of Balaam's prophecy about the star:

Seventy weeks are decreed
On your people and on your holy city...
To make an end of sins
To make reconciliation for iniquity
To bring in everlasting righteousness
To seal up vision and prophecy
To anoint the most holy
Know therefore and discern
That from the going forth of the commandment
To restore and to build Jerusalem
To the Anointed One, the prince
Shall be seven weeks, and sixty-two weeks...
After the sixty-two weeks
The Anointed One hall be cut off...
He shall make a firm covenant
With many for one week
In the midst of the week he shall cause
The sacrifice and the offering to cease...

Daniel 9:24-27

Malik's father, a priest of Jehovah, explained that in most prophecies, a day was symbolic of a year. So the "seven weeks and 62 weeks" were equal to 69 weeks or 483 days/years. After this time period, an important figure, called the Anointed One or *Meshicha*, would enter the world to end sin, reconcile man with Jehovah and bring an end to the current religious system. For some reason, Malik thought of the prophecy of Balaam and felt that both must be talking about the same event.

He also knew from studying some of the other documents preserved in the Damascus libraries, like the writings of the Hebrew Nehemiah, that the decree to rebuild Jerusalem was given to Nehemiah by the Persian king Artaxerxes. What Malik found astonishing was that the decree had been given 482 years before, which meant that the fulfillment of the prophecy was almost upon them!

Malik shared his findings with some of his friends who also got excited. Together they began to study the heavens in earnest to see if there might not be a cosmic, real fulfillment of the prophecy of the star. Amazingly, a few months later, as Malik went outside one night, he noticed a bright new star on the horizon! Sure this was the answer he was looking for, he hurried to tell his friends. After some quick deliberations, they decided to set out the next evening, heading in the direction of the star, and see where it led them.

So, that's how Malik now finds himself in the desert sleeping next to a camel. Of the 24 people who set out with him, only five remain: two friends, Kaab and Fihr and their three servants. They have four camels, three for riding and one for carrying the gifts they want to bring to the *Meshicha*: gold, frankincense and myrrh.

Malik had wanted absolutely to bring frankincense, but couldn't find any in the markets along the Euphrates, so they'd been forced to travel to southern Arabia to obtain some directly from the source. Of course, this trip had delayed their expedition by many months, and was one of the main reasons most of the others had abandoned ship.

After a few more sleepless hours, Malik and the rest get up, pack the skins and water bags back on the camels and slowly trudge through the twilight, following the star. After a few hours, they come over a hill and see the warm glow of thousands of lamps lighting up a city on a hill across the valley. They know from other travelers that they are in the vicinity of Jerusalem, and Malik is sure that this must be it.

Weary from over a year on the road, they find an inn and bed down for the night among the animals from several other caravans.

Early the next day, Malik rouses his companions and they set off through the city to see if anyone knows where the *Meshicha* might be found. Certainly, the Hebrews should know. After all, most of the prophets they've been studying were Hebrews. They are surprised when most people either brush them off with slight annoyance or look at them like they're lunatics.

As they leave yet another market and round a corner on a side street, a man comes out of the shadows and blocks their way.

"May peace be upon you, strangers," the man begins.

"And may peace be upon you," replies Malik with an air of curiosity.

"I overheard your inquiries. I think I can help. I know some of the leading priests and teachers of the prophecies here in Jerusalem. I can introduce you to them…for a small fee, of course."

Malik studies the man for a few seconds. While he seems a little shady, Malik isn't getting anywhere with his own methods, so he decides to take a risk.

"Here's two gold coins. Lead us to the right people and you'll get two more later."

"Follow me!" the man commands as he heads off down another narrow, cobblestoned road.

Climbing, turning, up and down the twisting, narrow streets of the ancient city, Malik soon realizes he is hopelessly lost, his life and the lives of his friends totally in the hands of a complete stranger. Instinctively, Malik clutches the hilt of the ever-present dagger just inside the folds of his robe. But he won't get a chance to use it.

Rounding one more corner, the group finds themselves suddenly face to face with a small cohort of Roman soldiers armed to the teeth. The soldiers quickly surround them while Malik's "guide" converses in hushed tones with the captain who slips him some coins and sends him on his way.

"You speak our language?" the captain asks in Latin. Malik had studied some Latin in school and can read Hebrew and Aramaic, but is mostly conversant in Persian, Arabic and Greek.

"I speak small, small," Malik fumbles in crude Latin. "But I'm much better in Greek…" He continues, switching languages.

"Fine, fine, no problem," the captain mutters back in Greek. "Come with me. King Herod has heard about you and invites you to see him in his palace. Sorry about that skunk who lead you here. We have to hire people like him who give us inside information. It makes our job easier to have an inside man. How much did he take you for?"

"Just a couple of gold coins. It's no big deal."

"Good…like I said, we're just doing our job. We have to know what's going on in this crazy city. It's not often we get anyone coming here from the East."

Malik and the captain continue to make small talk as they are lead through some narrow passages, several courtyards and many locked gates into the inner palace of the ruler of Jerusalem. They find Herod draped in leopard skin robes and seated on an enormous, gold plated throne.

"Your majesty, I've brought the visitors from the East who've been asking all the questions about the *Meshicha* in the markets." With that introduction, the captain motions Malik to step forward while he retreats with his men to the back of the audience room.

"May peace by upon you and your family, O great ruler," Malik bows his head respectfully and touches his heart with his right hand in a gesture of respect.

"And peace be upon you...what brings you to Jerusalem and what's all this I hear about a...what was it you called it? A *Meshicha*? Is that right?"

"Yes, your majesty. We have been studying some of the prophecies from ancient times and believe that there is some metaphysical appearance of a being called the *Meshicha* who, according to our calculations, should have appeared sometime last year. We have been following a new star that arose in our land, and the star has led us here. So we've been asking around to see if anyone knows anything about any unusually important births or any information on where we might find this extraordinary person, the *Meshicha*."

"I see, yes, yes, of course. I knew, of course, that you were here and that you were seeking this, uh, *Meshicha*, so I took the liberty of calling in our own local experts on these, uh, matters. You know, our scribes, priests and all the rest. And you'll be happy to know that they've informed me that this...*Meshicha* creature as you call it...should be born in Bethlehem. It's not far, you know, just down the road."

"Thank you, your grace, may the blessings of Jehovah fall upon you..."

"Fine, fine, off you go then." Herod signals the end of their audience with a lazy wave of his jeweled hand.

Malik and the others bow, turn to go and are almost out of the room when Herod stops them.

"Oh, there's one last thing...this is all very interesting you know. I am, in fact, a religious sort of person myself...all this is really quite fascinating and, uh, I would much appreciate it if you'd stop by the palace on your way back from Bethlehem...you know, just let me know how it went... maybe I can go and worship the, uh, *Meshicha*, too you know?"

"Certainly, O King," replies Malik courteously. "It would be our pleasure and the least we could do for your generous hospitality. May peace be upon you."

With the aid of a young soldier assigned to them as guide, Malik and his companions quickly find their way back to the inn where they left their camels. Within the hour they are outside the city gates on the narrow road to Bethlehem.

The road descends steeply into a valley and then a broad plain. Only five kilometers from Jerusalem, Bethlehem is more of a large village than a town. Stone huts with flat roofs huddle among the palm trees. The surrounding hillsides are covered with twisted olive groves. Roosters, chickens, goats, dogs and cats scurry about in search of whatever they can find to eat.

Malik stops at the large caravanserai on the edge of the village and greets some old, bearded men lounging in the shade of a tree, stretched out on a large mat woven from palm fronds.

"Peace be upon you," Malik greets them in Arabic.

"And may peace be upon you," the men chorus in Aramaic. Since Arabic is a close cousin of Aramaic, Malik continues in Arabic while the men reply in their native tongue.

"We're from the East and have traveled through Arabia following a new star. In studying our prophecies, and those of your Hebrew scriptures, we're convinced that *al-Masih*...er the *Meshicha*...was born sometime recently. We're looking for a child that was born a little over a year ago, possibly under unusual circumstances."

"Well," replies one of the old men after a long pause and looking at one of his companions. "Do you suppose it could be that carpenter and his wife? You know, the one who had a baby out in the shepherds' caves? Some of the local herders made a big deal out of it, talking about angels, and bright lights and such..."

"Yep, I bet that's the one. Names are Yosef and Maryam, good people, keep to themselves, real quiet and nice like."

"You can find them on the other side of town, just a little past the well, about a hundred feet after the big pile of rocks to your left."

"Thank you, may Jehovah's peace rest upon you, brothers." With that Malik salutes them with his right hand on his chest and moves on with the others.

Reaching the pile of rocks, they turn left and come upon a simple house built of stacked stones with split palm trunks supporting a thatched roof. The sun is going down and Malik isn't sure if he's imagining it or not, but it seems like their star is hovering over the simple dwelling. An ordinary man in a simple woven robe sits outside on a stool. Wood shavings are all around and Malik notices several partially finished chairs and a table under a small veranda made of woven mats to the side of the hut.

"Peace be upon you, stranger." The man greets Malik before he has a chance to give the traditional greeting.

"And peace be upon you..." Malik offers. Then after a brief hesitation, he adds, "...Yosef, husband of Maryam."

"I see you have the advantage in that you know my name while I know nothing of you."

"My name is Malik, these are my friends, Kaab and Fihr. We have come a great distance from the lands of the East near the Great River to see your child. We have followed a new star that arose according to the prophecies of Balaam, and it has guided us here. We also are familiar with your prophet, Daniel, and feel that your child is a fulfillment of his 69 week prophecy of *al-Masih*."

"Hold on a second. Maryam, come out here. You have to hear what these guys are saying!" Yosef calls inside the house. A short, slender girl of about 15 comes out the doorway, her head covered in a bright yellow scarf, carrying a small infant. "This is my wife, Maryam, and our son, Yeshua."

Malik then repeats to Maryam what he'd just told Yosef, adding in all the detail of their studies of the prophecies of Balaam, Daniel and Nehemiah, their journey through Arabia, their arrival in Jerusalem, the encounter with King Herod and how the star finally came to rest over this humble abode.

Maryam looks shyly up at Yosef who just keeps shaking his head in wonder. "Maryam, I think you better tell them your story. But first come sit with us. Maryam, bring some milk and tea. Please forgive us, we don't have much, but what we have is yours."

While Maryam goes inside to prepare the tea, Yosef spreads out a large mat in front of the house under the stars and the weary travelers sit down thankfully. Soon Maryam brings out the steaming teapot, several small cups, a bowl of fresh goat's milk, and some dried dates and olives on a platter.

As the men eat on the mat, Maryam sits to the side on Yosef's stool. When they have satisfied their hunger and thirst, she begins her story.

"I had just reached the age of marriage and my parents arranged with Yosef's family to have us meet. We each found the other agreeable so a bride price was soon fixed. Yosef is quite the carpenter," says Maryam as she glances admiringly at Yosef out of the corner of her eye. "So he had no problem paying the dowry and we were soon engaged.

"The date for the wedding was set for six months later. One day, I'd gone off by myself to pray. I had the habit of taking little spiritual retreats away from my family and I used to hide behind a little screen of palm fronds so that no one would see me. It was kind of silly, but it made me feel alone, yet safe.

"So, that one fateful day, I was off in my secret little place when a man appeared in front of me. I couldn't figure out how he'd gotten in and I didn't recognize him. I was terrified and blurted out the first thing that came to my mind, 'Jehovah, help me from this man if he doesn't fear you...' but before I could finish, the man held up his hand and interrupted me with a kind voice.

"'I am only a messenger from Jehovah, to announce to you the gift of a sinless son. O Maryam! Jehovah gives you the glad news of a Word from him, his name will be Yeshua *Meshicha* held in honor in this world and in the next, and will be one of those who are near to Jehovah. He will speak to the people in infancy and adulthood, and he will be one of the righteous.'

"So I asked him, 'How can I have a son, when no man has touched me, and I'm not unchaste?'

"The man, who I was beginning to suspect was an angel, replied 'That is easy for Jehovah. He wishes to appoint the boy as a sign to mankind and a mercy from Jehovah. It is a matter already decreed. So it will be. Jehovah creates what he wills. When he has decreed something, he says to it only: "Be!"—and it is.'

"Then the angel disappeared. I didn't know what to do, so I finished my prayers and went home. But when I realized I was pregnant a few months later, even though I was still a virgin, I had to tell Yosef. I hoped he would understand."

"Well, it was hard for me, I tell you," Yosef interrupts. "Here this girl is giving me this wild tale of being pregnant and claiming some angel had told her that it would be by some miracle of Jehovah, what was I supposed to think? I knew I hadn't touched her, so I as much as I hated to admit it, I had to believe she'd broken our vows. But I loved her and didn't want to embarrass her. Besides, if I denounced her to the authorities, they'd stone her for adultery. So I decided to divorce her quietly, without explaining why, and just let the family keep the dowry so I'd save her honor and her life.

"But before I could talk to anyone about it, I had a dream. A bright being, I can only assume it was an angel, came to me and told me clearly, 'Yosef son of David, do not be afraid to take Maryam home as your wife, because what is conceived in her is from the Holy Spirit. She will give birth to a son, and you are to give him the name Yeshua, because he will save his people from their sins.'

"What finally convinced me that all this must be true, despite how outrageous it sounds, is that up to this point, Maryam hadn't told me that the angel told her to name the boy, Yeshua. So when we compared notes and realized that the angel had told each of us the same name, we felt like it must be from Jehovah. So, I didn't divorce her. It was hard though, because when we got married, everyone could see that Maryam was pregnant. It was very shameful for both our families.

"In a way, I was relieved when we got the decree from the emperor for the census saying we all had to register in our home towns. I'm originally from here in Bethlehem, from the line of King David. With all the gossip in our hometown, I was only too happy to get out of Nazareth and come here.

"When we got here, though, after days of hard traveling, Maryam started to have contractions and I knew she was going to deliver soon. But we couldn't find any room anywhere. It seems King David has a lot of descendants and the town was overrun. We finally got shelter in one of the shepherds' caves out in the hills. I was scared. I'd never seen a baby be born before, but thankfully there were no complications.

"I cleaned him off with straw, wrapped him in rags and put him in a feed trough. Then, I helped Maryam clean up. I never knew deliveries were so messy and bloody!

"The strangest thing was, a few hours later, a bunch of herders came in with all their sheep and gathered around telling us a wild tale. Apparently, they were minding their own business, sitting around the fire telling jokes when a bright light came right overhead and temporarily blinded them. Then they saw a group of angels. One of them came up and spoke:

"'Do not be afraid, I bring you good news of great joy for all people. Today in Bethlehem was born a savior, who is the *Meshicha*. And this is how you'll recognize him: you will find a baby wrapped in rags, lying in a feed trough.'

"Then all the angels started singing, 'Glory to Jehovah in the highest, and on earth peace, goodwill toward men!'

"Then things kind of quieted down and we settled here in Bethlehem. I found work and we thought our lives had returned to normal. Until you arrived just now that is!"

Malik sits back. He realizes that he's been leaning forward with bated breath during the entire story. He lets out a low whistle. *This is too good to be true! After all those years of study and travel and uncertainty, here I am face to face with* al-Masih...*and he's an infant contentedly breastfeeding!*

"I feel the presence of Jehovah here," Malik slowly begins. "We would like to pray and bless the child. We have come a long way to see him and present him with our gifts."

With that, they all stand and face East, hands outstretched, eyes lifted to the sky as they recite their prayers to the God of Abraham. Then they unload the camel and present their gifts of gold, frankincense and myrrh. Yosef and Maryam are speechless, but take the gifts and hide them away in the house. Yosef arranges a place to the side where the guests can stretch out their rugs and sheepskins and everybody is soon fast asleep.

Malik has a nightmare. *He is back in Jerusalem. This time the streets are empty and a heavy darkness covers everything in shadows. He is transported to Herod's palace where he enters the audience room alone. A single fire blazes in a brazier to the side of the throne. Suddenly he hears a hissing and a large snake slithers its way toward him, it's tongue flicking in and out as it somehow manages to grin at him. Looking into the serpent's eyes, he recognizes the eyes of Herod...*

Waking up in a cold sweat, Malik tries to calm his racing heart. He knows instantly what the dream means: Herod is not to be trusted. Malik silently wakes the others and they begin to prepare the camels for a fast getaway. Just then, the door to the house opens and a wild-eyed Yosef bursts out.

"Sorry to…wait what's going on? Are you leaving…?"

"We have to. I've been warned in a dream that King Herod is not to be trusted, so we're getting out of here and returning to our land by the northern route to avoid Jerusalem."

"Are you serious? This is crazy! I also just had a similar dream. The same angel came to me again and told me that Herod is trying to kill Yeshua. He said we should flee to Egypt. Before you came, that would have been impossible, we're poor you know. But now…would you mind if we used the gold to…"

"Of course, of course," interrupts Malik as he cinches his camel's saddle tight. "In fact, take this fourth camel, you'll need it to cross the Sinai Peninsula. May Jehovah protect you and guard you and bless you. May peace be upon you."

With that, Malik swings into the saddle, the camel slowly rocks back and forth to its feet, and the group lumbers off silently into the night as Yosef quickly packs his things and sets off on the road to Egypt.

The two groups of people present at the miraculous birth of Jesus the Messiah (*Isa al-Masih* or *Yeshua Meshicha*), show once again the collaboration between the children of Isaac and the Children of the East. It also is a fulfillment of the sanctuary service that Moses inaugurated with the Israelites in the desert around Mount Sinai.

According to the law of Moses, every offering, whether it was grain or animal, should be accompanied by the burning of incense (frankincense). This incense was found in only one spot: southern Arabia. So from the earliest times of the Jewish economy all the way to the birth of Jesus, the two different Abrahamic lines had to cooperate for it to work. The incense came from the Children of the East, and the grain and animals came from the Children of Isaac.

So, when Jesus is born, shepherds from the hills surrounding Bethlehem come to worship him, bringing their sheep, and Wise Men from the East come following the prophecy of Balaam bringing frankincense and myrrh, fulfilling once again Jehovah's plan that the two groups should work together to accomplish Jehovah's purposes.

Jesus grows up in Egypt and then returns to Nazareth when King Herod dies. He fulfills Jehovah's destiny for his life by revealing the character of Jehovah to the world, going so far as to demonstrate the greatest love of all by letting himself be killed, rising up from the grave three days later and ascending to Jehovah's right hand. As Jesus himself says:

Greater love has no one than this
That someone lay down his life for his friends
You are my friends
If you do whatever I command you
No longer do I call you servants
For the servant doesn't know what his lord does
But I have called you friends
For everything that I heard from Jehovah
I have made known to you

John 15:13-15

After Jesus' resurrection, his early followers first gain some new members and then shortly after begin to be persecuted. The inquisition is led by a young religious leader named Saul, who, on his way to Damascus to arrest some of Jesus' followers, is about to have a life-changing experience...

Saul

Nor did I go up to Jerusalem
To those who were apostles before me
But I went away into Arabia
Then I returned to Damascus
Then after three years I went up to Jerusalem

Galatians 1:17-18

And remember how God...
Gave you a place to live on the earth:
You...carve out dwellings in the mountains...
Do you know Salih to be
An emissary from his Lord?
They said, "We are believers
In what was sent through him."

Qur'an 7:74-75

Saul wipes the sweat from his brow and shifts his simple goatskin bag to his other shoulder. *It's been a long day...no, it's been a long few weeks.* Ever since he entered the deserts of northern Arabia he has seen mile after endless mile of bare rock and sand with hardly anything green to break the monotony.

According to his map, though, he should be getting close to his destination. He grew up hearing stories about the wild desert people and their stone city, but they were so extraordinary, he always kind of assumed they were just tall tales. *I guess I'm about to find out now...*

He's been following this line of cliffs for miles now and according to the map, the secret entrance should be around here somewhere. His friend

Daoud from Damascus warned him that until he was right on top of it, he wouldn't see it, and if he wasn't paying attention, he'd miss it altogether.

Saul decides to take a break. Hovering against the meager shade of a rock, he pulls out his almost empty water skin and takes a slow drink from the warm, brackish contents. Wiping his beard, he closes his eyes for a few minutes rest. *It's hard to believe that just a year ago...* Saul's mind drifts back to the events that have led him to this point...

"Stone him!"

"He doesn't deserve to live..."

"What's his name?"

"Stephen...I think..."

"What'd he do...?"

"Claims we persecuted the prophets..."

"That we murdered and betrayed..."

"Says we even killed the *Meshicha*..."

"Outrageous!!!"

"Blasphemy!!!"

"Stone him! STONE Him!! STOOOOOHHHHNNNE HIM!!!"

Saul watched from a careful distance as the mob dragged the young man out the city gates to the trash pit. They quickly removed their outer cloaks so as not to stain them with blood and piled them at Saul's feet. Saul nodded his approval of their observance of the cleanliness laws. Then the crowd picked up stones and pounded the lad to death, his blood spattering the hard ground at the entrance to the garbage dump.

Saul starts to weep as his body is wracked with sobs. It seems like no matter how many times he relives the scene, he can't find peace. But crying does help some. His thoughts wander back to what happened just after the stoning...

"Your honor," Saul addressed the graying man in front of him as he bowed low. "I am requesting an official letter from the Sanhedrin authorizing me to weed out the heresy in Damascus. We have done well in all the towns surrounding Jerusalem and have put the blasphemers either in jail or have forced them to flee the country. But I hear that many of them have taken refuge in Damascus."

"As you know," replied the High Priest. "Damascus isn't even under Roman rule. King Aretas IV from the Nabataean Kingdom has taken it from the Romans and appointed his own governor. I'm not sure if he'll recognize..."

"Excuse me for interrupting, sir," interjected Saul. "But that's exactly why a letter from the Sanhedrin will carry more weight than the letters I already have from the Roman Consul. There is still a sizable Jewish population in Damascus and the governor will be eager to keep peace with the Jewish authorities..."

"I see your point...Well thought out...It's brilliant actually...I'll get right on it. Come back later this evening and you'll have what you need."

"Thanks, your grace. May Jehovah's blessings rest upon you and our people."

With that, Saul bowed and exited the Temple, making his way back to his house where he immediately ordered his donkeys packed and sent word to his men that their next mission had been approved.

The next morning, papers signed by the High Priest in hand, Saul and his warriors set out on the long road to Damascus. As they were nearing the city, suddenly an explosion of light literally knocked Saul off his donkey to the ground as his hands went instinctively to his eyes and face to try and protect himself.

"Saul, Saul, why are you persecuting me and my people?"

Afraid to look up, Saul kept his face to the ground and replied in a cracking voice, "Uh, who ARE you?

"I am Yeshua *Meshicha*, the same one whose followers you are throwing in prison. Now get up, go into the city and wait there for my command."

And just like that, the light was gone, leaving Saul in total darkness. He fumbled around, got up and tried to rub his eyes to clear them, believing that something had got on them or in them. That's when he realized he could no longer see...he was blind!

"Hey, somebody help me..."

"Saul, Saul, we're right here," replied one of his men grabbing him by the shoulders and shaking him as if to waken him out of a dream. "What's going on? Why are you talking to yourself?"

"What? Didn't you see...? Am I going crazy? There was this light and...never mind, never mind. Let's get going into the city. I can't see. Help me on my donkey."

Stunned and not sure what to do or say the men were relieved to have Saul back giving orders and quickly complied. It was a somber group that made their way through the gates of Damascus later that afternoon. Saul had planned on staying with a friend named Judas who lived on Straight Street so his men took him there and dropped him off. They then continued on to the central synagogue where they would be lodged.

"Peace be upon you, Judas my friend," greeted Saul as he held out a wavering hand searching for the hand he hoped was extended to him.

"Excuse me, but the weirdest thing has happened. I'll explain later, but suffice it to say, I suddenly became blind today, so I'll need some help."

"Sure, sure, come on in," assured Judas as he reached out to guide his friend into his house. "And peace be upon you, as well."

The next three days were the longest of Saul's life as he was forced to reevaluate everything he had stood for over the last ten years. He had been trained by the best Jewish theologian of the time, Gamaliel, and had become the strictest of the strict, a Pharisee of Pharisees. He had thrown into prison countless followers of the Way, as the disciples of Yeshua called themselves. Now, to think that he may have missed the greatest event in history, the coming of the *Meshicha*, and not only missed it, but been on the side of *Meshicha*'s enemies was more than Saul's brain could handle.

He couldn't sleep and decided to go on a fast. For three days he spent the entire time praying and crying his eyes out, seeking for answers. Slowly but surely, all those scriptures that he'd memorized started to make more sense. He realized that they were all pointing to and fulfilled in the life of Yeshua. But what did Jehovah want with him now?

Just then, there was a knock on the door. He heard Judas' footsteps cross the room to the door.

"Peace be upon you, brother." A deep, unknown voice echoed into the room from the street.

"And peace be upon you," replied the well-known voice of Judas. "How can I help you?"

"I've been sent by Jehovah to find a man named Saul who I was told is staying on Straight Street with a man named Judas. Someone pointed out to me that this is Judas' house. Are you Judas?"

"Yes, that's me." Saul sensed a note of surprise in Judas' voice. "Come on in. I'll go get Saul now."

Saul stumbled to his feet and was grateful for the shoulder of Judas to guide him into the room where he heard a man's coarse breathing and heavy footsteps move toward him. Then he felt the man's strong hands grasp both of his shoulders. They stood in silence for what seemed like hours as Saul felt a warm presence fill his heart.

"Brother Saul, yesterday I had a dream where Yeshua told me to come find you at this address and that you would have had a dream that a man named Ananias would come help you recover your vision."

"Yes, that's true," exclaimed Saul breathlessly. "Are you...?"

"Yes, I'm Ananias. Receive your sight in the name of Yeshua *Meshicha*!"

Immediately, Saul felt something like scales fall off his eyes and he found himself looking into the wizened, bearded face of a man with a huge smile on his face and a twinkle in his eye. As Ananias realized Saul could see, he quickly embraced him in a bear hug and the two rocked back and forth pounding each other's backs as Saul sobbed and sobbed.

As a strange warmth poured through him, Saul opened his mouth to praise Jehovah, but found himself speaking in another language that he would later learn was Arabic.

"Bismillah ar-rachman ar-rahim, al hamdullilah rabbi al amin, ar-rachman ar-rahim, maliki yawmi din, iyaka naabudu wa iyaka nasta-eem..."

And with that Paul fell prostrate before Jehovah and worshipped.

Saul sits up, grabs his bag and stands to his feet. Shading his eyes he scans the horizon. Nothing, as far as the eye can see. He turns and continues following the rock wall to his right. There it is! A tiny crack in the face extending up and out of sight. It's barely wide enough for a donkey to squeeze through. He slips into the shadows and finds himself in a windy passageway headed who knows where.

The floor is flat and covered with fine sand. Above, he can see just a glimmer of blue sky which has no hope of reaching the bottom of the chasm. He moves slowly forward. Ahead, there is a sharp turn. As he rounds the corner...

Suddenly, a blur of red and brown rushes at him from both sides. Saul quickly finds himself with his back in the sand, blood in his mouth, a knife at his throat and a spear tip poking his belly. Two dark, fierce eyes blaze out at him from a face completely obscured by a white turban wrapped in multiple layers around a head, masking the assailant's identity.

"Who are you and what do you want? Be quick or your death will be even quicker." The man speaks in Aramaic with a heavy Arabic accent.

"I'm Saul, a friend of King Aretas IV," Paul replies in Arabic. "I come from Damascus to seek refuge with him from my enemies."

A look of surprise widens Saul's attacker's eyes as he slowly lifts the blade from Saul's neck. He stands up and sheathes the sword as his companion pulls up his spear and leans casually on it, one leg doubled up with its foot resting on the opposite leg's inner thigh like a flamingo.

"So, show me some papers. The King told us about you, but we need proof."

"Here," Paul reaches slowly into his bag and pulls out an oilskin with the precious documents inside. The guard scans them rapidly and hands them back.

"Okay, follow me."

The two men set a brisk pace and Saul struggles to follow. As they walk, the men are curious to know how a Jew became friends with their king and how he ended up out here in their desert stronghold.

"Well, it's a long story," begins Saul. "I was sent to Damascus by the Jewish leaders in Jerusalem to hunt out some heretics called the followers of the Way. They believed that *al-Masih* had come..."

When Saul mentions the name *al-Masih* the two men give him a curious look but then motion him to continue.

"...And that his name was Yeshua or Isa in your language. They had this crazy story that he'd been raised from the dead. I myself had seen him be crucified by the Romans, so I found that hard to believe. I figured they must be heretics and needed to be stopped from spreading lies around and dividing our people.

"So I started hunting them down and throwing them in prison. I was even the ringleader of a mob that stoned one of them to death: a young man named Stephen. I'll never forget the look of peace and joy as he lifted his eyes to heaven. His face seemed to glow as we bashed his brains out.

"But I quickly shook that off and after imprisoning or running out of town pretty much all the other followers of this Isa, I decided to continue my work in Damascus. When I was almost there, I was blinded by an explosion of light and a voice from heaven saying that I was persecuting him. Who are you? I asked. 'Isa *al-Masih*,' the voice replied.

"I was completely blind and spent three days fasting and praying, searching my soul and trying to find forgiveness. Then a man named Ananias came, put his hands on me, prayed in the name of Isa *al-Masih* and I could see again!

"Immediately, I started going to the synagogues and telling the other Jews that I had found *al-Masih* and his name was Isa. Well, as you can imagine, that didn't go over too well. Soon I was brought before the governor of Damascus. Since I had introductory papers from Jerusalem, the governor interviewed me in private.

"'I believe what you're saying,' he said. 'But politically, I can't support you. The Jews are too powerful here. I must warn you, they are putting guards at all the gates, and as soon as you step foot outside the city, they'll nab you.'

"'So here's what I suggest.' continued the governor. 'I'm going to give you an introductory letter to my king, Sultan Aretas IV. He lives in our stronghold in the Arabian desert, a town called Petra. Its location is secret, but I'll draw you a map. He will provide protection and will be happy to receive you. There are a few of us who have continued to worship the God of Abraham, even though most also worship other gods.'

"'Get out of town anyway you can, and then head out to the Negev and follow my map. When you enter the secret passageway, present yourself as the Sultan's friend and give him this letter from me. I'll also send word so he'll be expecting you. Peace be upon you.'

"And with that, I was escorted secretly out of the governor's palace and made my way back to a safe house. There, I explained to the brothers that the Jews were trying to kill me. One of them had a house that was built into the wall. So they put me in a large basket and lowered me out the window, down the wall and to the ground. It was pitch dark with no moon so I made an easy getaway and hit the road for the desert that very night.

"I've been searching for this place for the last three weeks and, praise be to the God of Abraham, I have finally found you."

The men seem satisfied with Saul's story and the rest of the trip is spent in silence. They wind their way through what seems like miles of narrow passageways with channels cut in the sides to funnel water into the mountain. Finally, rounding the last corner, Saul finds himself face to face with one of the wonders of the ancient world.

He's heard of the Edomite capital, Sela, at Mount Seir, but the sight is beyond anything he could have imagined. Across a huge courtyard, open to the desert sky is another cliff. Carved into the cliff is a four story building with pillars and reliefs that rival anything he's seen in the Roman world, except that this is over 700 years old and has been carved out of solid rock.

They enter the courtyard which reveals itself to be a long valley whose walls are lined with different buildings and houses chiseled out of the stone. Petra is a bustling city that just fades into the mountain.

They hurry across to the treasury building, climb the stairs and enter a cavernous doorway into the inner room. As his eyes adjust to the darkness, Saul notices he is in the audience chamber. A throne stands right before him, cut out of rock with lions and ibexes carved in and around the seat.

On the throne sits a lean, weathered man who could be anywhere from 30 to 70 years old. He seems ageless. He wears a simple bedouin robe and rough leather sandals. The only thing that distinguishes him as king is his richly embroidered black turban with a large gem set in the center of the forehead.

"Welcome to Petra, or Sela as it has been called." Aretas motions for Saul to move forward. "May peace be upon you."

"And upon you be peace, O Sultan," exclaims Saul, bowing slightly and touching his right hand to his heart.

"Come, walk with me," says Aretas. "Let me tell you a little of our history."

Aretas takes Saul along a narrow path hugging the edge of a cliff about 40 feet high where they can see the whole of the ancient stone city splayed out before them.

"Back in the early days of the Edomite kingdom, after the deaths of their first two kings, Balaam son of Beor and Job from the land of Uz, the descendants of Esau felt they needed a more secure location for their capital. They wandered around Mount Seir for years before someone discovered the secret passageways into the heart of this mountain fortress.

"They began to carve out the city, starting with the palace we just left and little by little their people moved from the plains to the mountains. They never lost their love of the nomadic life and the open flatlands though. So as soon as the Babylonians took the Jews from Jerusalem and razed the city to the ground a little over 600 years ago, many of the Edomites moved back into the vacuum created by the diaspora, and started herding again on the grasslands of Judah.

"At about the same time, our ancestors, the Rechabites, led by Jaazaniah the Maakathite, left Jerusalem on the advice of the prophet Jeremiah. Jeremiah had long predicted the fall of Jerusalem to the Babylonians, but the Rechabites were one of the few to listen to him and they got out just in time.

"Being nomads themselves before fleeing Jerusalem, our people knew the deserts around here well. Looking for a place safe from the Babylonians they wandered here to Petra where they found the place almost abandoned by the Edomites. We moved in and slowly but surely, other Arabs joined us. We all intermarried until we became one people. The Arabs call us the Nabataeans because we originally spoke Aramaic from Jerusalem. However, over the years, with all the influence from the southern Arab tribes, we have come to speak Arabic, although most of us understand and speak Aramaic as well.

"The main thing that has happened with time is that we have started worshipping the gods of the desert tribes. I myself grew up worshipping many idols. But on my travels to Damascus, I came across a scroll by the prophet Jeremiah that told the story of how my ancestors, the Rechabites worshipped Jehovah, the one true God, the Creator of the heavens and the earth.

"Since that time, I have prayed only to Jehovah, but still do not know much about him. Then, some of our people were in Jerusalem and heard some simple fishermen from Galilee talking in perfect Arabic telling them that *al-Masih* had come and that his name was Isa. They came back telling stories of miracles and healings. I told my governor in Damascus, if he ever finds a teacher who can teach our people the old ways, the religion of Abraham, and about *al-Masih,* that he should send him to us.

"That's why when I got his letter, I was so excited that he had found a true rabbi who could teach us the ways of Jehovah and of Isa. So, brother Saul, I have arranged a meeting for you to teach our people tomorrow in the great amphitheater over there."

Saul looks across the valley and sees a huge stadium carved out of the rock. Inside, he feels peace. This is the work of Jehovah. He was chased out of one place, only to find fertile ground in another. He knows this is his mission from above, to tell the truth about Jehovah as revealed in *Yeshua Meshicha*. This is what he was meant to do.

Saul stays three years in Petra. While there, he learns how to make tents which becomes a useful trade on some of his other missionary journeys. Most of the Nabataeans think he's crazy and keep on in idolatry. But there is a small group of believers who come back to the worship of the one true God. They call themselves the *hunafa*.

In 106 AD, the Romans finally conquer the Nabataeans who become part of the Roman province of Arabia. However, the story of the Rechabites doesn't end with the fall of Petra and the Nabataean kingdom. In 1839, a missionary by the name of Joseph Wolff finds in Arabia, near Makkah, a tribe claiming to be descendants of Jonadab. In the late nineteenth century a Bedouin tribe is discovered near the Dead Sea who also professes to be descended from the Rechabites.

So, the promise made to the Rechabites by Jehovah through the prophet Jeremiah is kept alive by the *hunafa* who never slip into idolatry and maintain their faithfulness through the centuries to the God of Abraham. One day in 610 AD, a young *hanif* named Ahmad goes up to a cave one evening to fast and pray...

Revelation

They were told that
They should not hurt the grass of the earth
Neither any green thing, neither any tree
But only those people who don't have
God's seal on their foreheads.

Revelation 9:4

Wretched is that for which
They have sold their soul,
That they would disbelieve
In what God has revealed,
Too conceited to admit
That God may cause
Divine blessing to descend
Upon any devotees that God wills.

Qur'an 2:90

The streets of Makkah are deserted. A slim crescent of a moon is all that lights the darkened alleyways. A warm desert breeze wafts across the rooftops as a dark figure moves quickly from shadow to shadow toward the outskirts of town. As the man reaches the sands of the desert, whose fingers seem to barely be held at bay from completely invading the ancient oasis, he pauses and looks back over his shoulder.

Tears fill his eyes as he remembers all that has happened over the last few years to lead him to this point. He loves this city and the thought of having to flee breaks his heart. The man turns back to the desert and raises his arms, palms upward as his soul prays to the one true God and his lips mouth the well-known words:

In the name of God, the beneficent, the merciful

Ahmad has always been a believer in the God of Abraham, a *hanif* as the Arabs call him. He was taught by his grandfather, Abd ul-Muttalib, who had received it from his father and on down the line. Ahmad's family could trace their lineage all the way back to the Nabataeans, the Rechabites, Ishmael, Abraham and finally Adam.

This knowledge of the One God who was the Creator of the heavens and the earth and the stories of all his prophets had been passed down around a thousand campfires until reaching Ahmad's ears as a young orphan raised by his grandpa.

But things really change when Ahmad started to fast and pray in earnest. He would retreat to a cave surrounding Makkah at least once a year and spend several days prostrated before the God of Abraham pleading to know more about him and seeking for his will.

When he was 40 years old, Ahmad was on one of these spiritual retreats when suddenly he felt the breath squeezed right out of him and heard a voice telling him to recite the words of the One God who was man's Creator. Frightened by the experience he returned home immediately to his wife, Khadidja, who comforted him and reassured him the message must be from the God of Abraham.

Ahmad started to receive many such messages and slowly began to share them, first with his family and then with others who were interested in reform. The descendants of Ishmael, the Children of the East, had almost completely forgotten the one true God and had turned to idolatry worshipping at least 360 gods in Makkah alone. Ahmad started telling people that they should worship the Creator God, the God of Abraham and that they should prepare for the final judgement. This was the essential message of the book which came to be called in Arabic *al-Qur'an.*

This reflects one of God's final warnings to the world as found in the first angel's message:

> *Fear Jehovah, and give him glory*
> *For the hour of his judgment has come*
> *Worship him who made the heaven, the earth,*
> *The sea, and the springs of waters!*

Revelation 14:7

As Ahmad stands on the edge of the desert that evening in 622 AD, little does he know that ten years later, at the time of his death, all of the warring Arabian tribes will be united under the banner of the worship of the God of Abraham, having completely abandoned polytheism and destroyed their idols.

Even more surprising to Ahmad would have been the fact that within 150 years, this reform movement would have spread across the Middle East into Central Asia and across North Africa into Spain. This crescent of Islam effectively encircled the Roman Church in Europe, keeping it from spreading to the rest of the world. In order to understand why this was a fulfillment of the Divine plan, we need to go back in history.

When the Romans came to power in the 3rd and 2nd centuries BC, they destroyed much of Greek civilization. They soon expanded their empire to include North Africa, Asia Minor and southern Europe. The Greek tradition of learning was disrupted, scholars killed and cities destroyed.

In the early fourth century AD, Constantine, who had already become Christian, acceded to Roman power. Christianity now became the state religion. Non-Christians were persecuted, burned at the stake and murdered by animated Christian mobs called zealots. Mathematicians, scientists and philosophers were particularly targeted. Europe was entering into an era called the Dark Ages with complete elimination of all the works of science, mathematics and philosophy. Even the Greek manuscripts of the New Testament were being burned. The official church position was that Latin was the only language to be used in liturgy and Bible study.

However, some knowledge of Greek, including a few copies of the Greek scriptures, were preserved at the University of Alexandria which was surviving still in Egypt. In 412 AD, a fanatic Christian named Cyril became the patriarch of Alexandria and began the campaign to rid the city of both Jews and the Greek scholars.

In 529 AD, the Byzantine Emperor Justinian completely destroyed the last remains of Greek knowledge in Europe by closing the 900-year-old Academy of Plato. Many Greek scholars, fearing for their lives and intellectual freedom fled to Persia, where they established a kind of Academy in exile.

Despite the attacks of fanatical Christians like Cyril, the Alexandrian school survived for another 200 years until the arrival of the Muslims. Some of the Greek scholars of Alexandria who embraced Islam were able to smuggle some of the Greek manuscripts to their homes. Later they translated these into Arabic. These translations included Greek medicine, much of Greek philosophy, and the Greek New Testament.

Meanwhile, in Europe all of the ancient Greek manuscripts of medicine, philosophy, science, and religion (including the Greek New Testament) were already burned to ashes by the Christian zealots. The end of knowledge in the West was complete. Fortunately for the true believers,

Islam had preserved the original copies of the New Testament so they couldn't be corrupted. Almost a thousand years later, it was the rediscovery of these scriptures and their translation that sparked Europe to come out of the Dark Ages with the Protestant Reformation, the Renaissance and the Enlightenment.

Those Christians who, during the Dark Ages wanted to escape the persecutions in Europe in order to worship God according to conscience and the scriptures, found refuge in Islamic lands to practice their faith. So Islam was a deliverance for God's people, while at the same time hurting and containing the apostasy in Europe.

All of this was predicted in the Revelation of Jesus Christ:

The fifth angel sounded, and I saw a star
From the sky which had fallen to the earth
The key to the pit of the abyss was given to him
He opened the pit of the abyss
And smoke went up out of the pit
Like the smoke from a burning furnace
The sun and the air were darkened
Because of the smoke from the pit.

Then out of the smoke
Came forth locusts on the earth
And power was given to them
As the scorpions of the earth have power
They were told that they should
Not hurt the grass of the earth
Neither any green thing, neither any tree
But only those people who
Don't have God's seal on their foreheads.

They were given power not to kill them
But to torment them for five months
Their torment was like the torment of a scorpion
When it strikes a person
In those days people will seek death
And will in no way find it
They will desire to die
And death will flee from them.

The shapes of the locusts
Were like horses prepared for war

On their heads were something like golden crowns
And their faces were like people's faces
They had hair like women's hair
And their teeth were like those of lions
They had breastplates, like breastplates of iron
The sound of their wings was like the sound of chariots
Or of many horses rushing to war.

They have tails like those of scorpions, and stings
In their tails they have power
To harm men for five months
They have over them as king
The angel of the abyss
His name in Hebrew is "Abaddon,"
But in Greek, he has the name "Apollyon."

Revelation 9:1-11

The English word *abyss* comes from the Greek word *abyssus* meaning deep, bottom, or chaos: in other words, a desolate area. In Genesis chapter one it refers to the surface of the world before creation when the Holy Spirit hovered over it. In Revelation 20 it means the earth after the plagues and destruction of the last days where Satan will be confined for a 1,000 years.

Out of the abyss come locusts. The most common swarming locust is the desert locust, which originates in desolate places. In southern Arabia is one of the most desolate places on earth called *Rub' al Khali* or the Empty Quarter. *Rub' al Khali* just happens to be where many locusts come from before swarming across the Indian subcontinent and Africa.

The angel of the Abyss is also mentioned elsewhere in Revelation:

I saw an angel coming down out of heaven
Having the key of the abyss...
He seized...the devil and Satan...
And bound him for a thousand years,

Revelation 20:1-2

Many people feel that since the angel with the key to the abyss in Revelation 9:1 fell to the earth that it must be referring to Satan or one of his angels. However, in Revelation 20:1-2, we have to ask the question is this angel on God's side or the enemy's? If he's binding the devil and Satan

111

and confining him to the desolate earth he can't be on Satan's side. So even though the angel with the key to the abyss in Revelation 9:1 is fallen from the sky, he must be working for God.

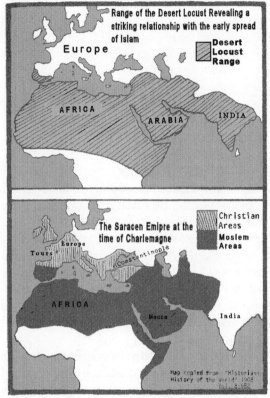

So it is logical that these verses are talking about Arabia. The description of the locusts in the later verses as horses, with long hair and breast plates also fits very well the historical description of the Muslim armies. In fact, most of the early Christian reformers like Martin Luther, John Calvin, Albert Barnes, John Wesley, Charles Spurgeon, Joseph Mede, John Napier, Sir Isaac Newton, and Jonathan Edwards were convinced that these verses could only be referring to Muhammad and the Arabs.

However, most Christians have assumed through the ages that these symbols indicating the rise of Islam were negative and harmful to the cause of God.

The main reason for this is that the last three trumpets (5th, 6th and 7th) are also called the three woes.

I saw, and I heard
An eagle flying in mid heaven
Saying with a loud voice
"Woe! Woe! Woe!
For those who dwell on the earth
Because of the other voices
Of the trumpets of the three angels
Who are yet to sound!"

Revelation 8:13

When most people hear the word *woe,* they think something like, "whoa, that's bad." But in order to understand what the Bible means by woe, we need to look at the third woe first.

> *The second woe is past*
> *Behold, the third woe comes quickly.*
> *The seventh angel sounded*
> *And great voices in heaven followed, saying*
> *"The kingdom of the world has become*
> *The kingdom of our Lord, and of his Christ*
> *He will reign forever and ever!"*

Revelation 11:14-15

These verses are clearly referring to the second coming of Jesus the Messiah. Is that event good or bad news for the true believers? Is it a woe to the people of faith? No, it's a deliverance from their enemies. Who is it a woe to? Those who have persisted in their rebellion against the God of Abraham and refused to submit to his will or be changed by his mercy and grace. They have reason to cry out "woe is me!" They will suffer the consequences of their poor choices. It is surely a woe to them.

So, the principle we can learn is that the 5th, 6th and 7th trumpets are all deliverances for the true believers, and judgments (woes) to the enemies of the God of Abraham who reject his mercy and grace.

In that case, in looking more carefully at the first woe, we can see this principle confirmed. The locusts are told to do what locusts don't usually do. Normally, locusts descend on a land and devour everything in site. They destroy. But here they are told to "not hurt the grass of the earth, neither any green thing, neither any tree, but only those people who don't have God's seal on their foreheads." They are also "given power not to kill... but to torment..."

In other words, these locusts are discriminating. Those who follow the God of Abraham aren't harmed by the locusts, only those who have apostatized. But even then, the unbelievers aren't destroyed, only hurt. We can see in history that the early spread of Islam across Arabia, the Middle East, North Africa and into Spain really didn't destroy Christian Europe, but it did hurt it in the sense that the apostasy was unable to spread outside the limits of the continent.

It was also a deliverance for the true believers by preserving the Greek manuscripts of the Bible, ensuring that corruption couldn't creep in. It guaranteed that the same scriptures that were originally written a long time ago are still available to us today. The crescent of Islam also contained the apostasy, inhibiting the spread of its violent suppression of freedom of religion from going to the rest of the world. Finally, Islam provided a place of refuge for those who differed from the teachings of the Roman Church and wanted to worship God according to their conscience and the scriptures.

The Arab Muslim conquests started after Muhammad's death in 632 AD and by 150 years later, in 782 AD, the capital of the new Islamic empire had moved to Baghdad where they entered a time of relative peace and prosperity. In Biblical prophecy, a day is equal to a year. So the five months of Revelation 9:10 is equal to five 30 day periods, or 150 days/years.

Revelation 9:11 says that these locusts, or the Arab armies, have as king over them the angel of the abyss. Angel is a transliteration of the Greek *angelos* meaning messenger. As we've seen, in this passage, *abyss* signifies Arabia. So the verse could be translated: "They have over them as king the messenger of Arabia." One of the popular titles of Muhammad is the messenger of Arabia.

In this same verse, the messenger of Arabia is said to have the Hebrew name *Abaddon* and the Greek name *Apollyon*. Both words mean destroyer or destruction. On first glance, this would appear to confirm most Christians' opinion of Muhammad: he is evil, the destroyer.

However, in looking at the preceding verses it is clear that the locust armies led by the messenger of Arabia didn't destroy, they only tormented or hurt. In fact, they are deliberately told not to destroy those having the seal of God. So what does this mean?

First of all, why would the verse put the name destroyer in two different languages and specifically say "in Hebrew...in Greek..."? The Revelation of Jesus Christ was originally written in Greek so why didn't he just say the *angelos* of the *abyssus* has the name *Apollyon*?

At that time period, most Christians spoke Greek and the language of the Jews was Hebrew. In other words, the writer of Revelation is saying that to the Christians and Jews at the time of Muhammad, the Arab armies would be seen as a destructive force aligned against them. But it must be recognized that the majority of those Christians and Jews had apostatized, were living in the Dark Ages and needed to be contained so that God's true people could be delivered.

The second woe also refers to Islam, this time in the form of the Ottoman Empire of the Turks.

The first woe is past
Behold, there are still two woes coming after this
The sixth angel sounded

I heard a voice from the horns
Of the golden altar which is before God
Saying to the sixth angel who had one trumpet
"Free the four angels who are bound
At the great river Euphrates!"
The four angels were freed
Who had been prepared for that
Hour and day and month and year
So that they might kill one third of mankind
The number of the armies of the horsemen
Was two hundred million
I heard the number of them

Thus I saw the horses in the vision
And those who sat on them having breastplates
Of fiery red, hyacinth blue, and sulfur yellow
And the heads of lions
Out of their mouths proceed
Fire, smoke, and sulfur
By these three plagues
Were one third of mankind killed
By the fire, the smoke, and the sulfur
Which proceeded out of their mouths
For the power of the horses is
In their mouths, and in their tails
For their tails are like serpents
And have heads, and with them they harm

The rest of mankind
Who were not killed with these plagues
Didn't repent of the works of their hands
That they wouldn't worship demons
And the idols of gold, and of silver
And of brass, and of stone, and of wood
Which can neither see, nor hear, nor walk
They didn't repent of their murders
Nor of their sorceries
Nor of their sexual immorality
Nor of their thefts.

Revelation 9:12-21

After several hundred years of living in fragile peace alongside the Muslims, the Christians decided to invade the Holy Land and retake Jerusalem. Thus began the Crusades and the beginning of real hostilities between the People of the Book (*Ahl al-Kitab*) and the followers of Muhammad.

As a reaction, the Muslims, represented in Revelation 9:14-17 by four angels coming from the Euphrates River area, leading a huge army of horsemen, swept out of Mesopotamia and retook Jerusalem under the direction of Saladin.

Hundreds of years had passed as Muslims and Christians lived side by side. What did the Muslims see? Did they see a Christlike, elevating life of a people committed to and serving God? No! They saw every abomination practiced by Christians. Fighting and feuding among Christians was constant. Muslims were convinced their religion was better and the Christians were infidels.

Osman, a Turkish emir, began uniting Muslims under what would become the Ottoman Empire. From 1300 AD onward, the Turks made serious inroads into Byzantine lands. The eastern Christian population began to panic as the Turks took over the countryside.

Yet, even now other Christian countries, rather than rallying to help, seemed more interested in getting their advantage from the greatly weakened Byzantine Empire. The Catalans first offered to help the Byzantines. Eventually, however, they joined the Turks in destroying and capturing Byzantine lands. Civil wars further weakened the Empire. The Turks were swarming in with little resistance.

The Byzantine emperor, John V, sought help from the pope, again promising the reunion of the eastern church under the western church. While he was in Rome, the Turks advanced through the Balkans. On his return in 1371 AD, John V meekly became a vassal of the Turkish emir, Murad. By 1391 AD the shrunken Byzantium empire consisted of Constantinople and a few nearby ports and islands. The Turks had taken most everything else.

Constantinople almost fell to the Turks in 1394 AD, when the emperor refused a new summons from the sultan. The Ottomans blockaded Constantinople, but due to their own problems they pulled the army away again, giving Constantinople a moment of reprieve. Finally, in 1430 AD the west became alarmed at the progress of the Muslims, and Pope Martin V began talking about reunion of the churches with the prospect of another crusade to drive back the Turks. But he died before anything was organized.

In 1443 AD, Pope Eugenius began preparations for a crusade. This raised the hopes of the Christians and some rebelled against the Turks. The crusaders battled the Turks at Varna, but were defeated. However, they had inflicted considerable damage to the Turkish army.

Constantine XI had fought against the Turks during the crusade. When the emperor, John VIII died in 1449 AD, Constantine inherited the throne. Yet he postponed his coronation until he made a new truce with the Turk, Murad II, who accepted him as a vassal. For many historians, this was the turning point. The emperor in Constantinople publicly showing that he could not rule till the Muslim leader sanctioned it!

In the *Millerite Signs of the Times* of February 01, 1840, Josiah Litch wrote the following interpretation of the 6th Trumpet of Revelation 9:

"The four angels denote ministers of judgment. They refer to the four nations of the Seljukan Turks of which the Ottoman empire was composed, located near the river Euphrates, at Aleppo, Iconiom, Damascus, and Bagdad. Up to the period of 1449 they had indeed tormented the Christian empire but could not subject it. When the sixth trumpet sounded, God seems to have overawed the Greek emperor, and all power of independence seems, as in a moment, to have fled...

"The number of horsemen were two hundred thousand thousand; what this number means, expositors have been at a loss to determine. But I am inclined to believe...that it means two hundred thousand twice told, making 400,000, in all. What makes this probable, is the fact, that the Turks usually had from three to four hundred thousand horsemen in their army. They had, when Constantinople was taken, three hundred thousand, and some say, four hundred thousand horsemen....

"Since the fifth trumpet sounded, there has been an astonishing change in the arms of the Turks. They, then had breastplates of iron, and were armed with dirks and scimitars. Now the scene is changed, and they are prepared with breastplates of fire, and of jacinth and brimstone. And out of the mouths of the horses, proceeded fire, smoke, and brimstone. Their power was in their mouth and tail; their tails were like serpents; long, cylindrical instruments like serpents with heads in them (bullets) with which they did hurt. This description has long been considered by expositors as a description of fire arms and gunpowder. And, indeed, I do not know how any one who knew nothing of such instruments could describe them more clearly.

"The design of these plagues is stated in the twentieth verse. It was to lead the people on whom these plagues were inflicted, to repent of their sins and break them of devil worship, etc. But they did not repent, neither of their murders, nor their sorceries, nor fornications, nor of their thefts. They, like most on whom the judgments of God fall, remain impenitent to this day; and the Turks continue to oppress them.

"But when will this power be overthrown?...The hour, fifteen days, the day, one year, the month, thirty years, and the year, three hundred and sixty years; in all, three hundred and ninety-one years and fifteen days, will end in A. D. 1840, some time in the month of August."

In other words, the Ottoman Empire, which really was given its true power in 1449 AD when Constantine XI became the vassal of the Turkish Emperor Murad II, would have its power until August 1840. During this time period, the Ottomans did not only contain the apostasy in Europe, but made inroads into the continent, conquering all the way to Vienna before being turned back.

Once again, the Muslims were a woe to the enemies of God. But how did they deliver God's people and accomplish God's purposes? Around this time, certain men of God in Europe were starting to try and reform the Christian church by getting back to the Bible. One of the leaders of this movement was a monk named Martin Luther. He translated the Bible into German making it available to the masses.

At the Diet of Spires in 1529 AD, the German princes stood up and defended the reform movement. Their protest is what gave the movement the name the Protestant Reformation. Charles V, the Roman Emperor, was determined to crush the rebellion against the Church. However, every time he gathered an army together to attack Luther and his German prince protectors, the Ottomans would attack Europe from the south and he would be obliged to leave the reformers alone to defend himself against the Muslims.

Therefore, thanks to Islam, those descendants of the Children of the East, the Protestant Reformation was left to strengthen and extend. Without this deliverance, Christian Europe would have been left in the Dark Ages.

The end of the second woe came as predicted. In 1839 Egypt captured Turkey's naval fleet and decimated its army. With only three ships left and a greatly weakened army, the Ottoman Empire would soon have been in the hands of the Egyptians, but England, Russia, Austria and Prussia came to Turkey's assistance. They forced Egypt to return the fleet to the Ottomans.

The weakened Ottoman Empire legally admitted that their existence depended upon the support of Christian nations when this ultimatum took effect, as it was hand delivered to the Egyptians by the Turkish envoy on August 11, 1840. The Turkish Sultan then watched the dismemberment of his weakened Empire as his protectors appropriated parts of his dominion for their own use, piece by piece.

Once again, the Children of Isaac and the Children of the East collaborated to bring about deliverances for God's people to accomplish his purposes for this world. But what about after the fulfillment of the prophecy of Revelation 9 that ended in 1840? It seems like the two lines of believers are on an unavoidable collision course rather than one of collaboration. Especially since September 11, 2001, it seems as if reconciliation and cooperation is impossible. Rather we see suicide bombings, terrorism, picketing, burning of Qur'ans, aggression, invasion, and hate.

Even if the descendants of Isaac and the descendants of Ishmael really are enemies today, neither group seems to be following the recommendations of Jesus:

You have heard that it was said
'You shall love your neighbor, and hate your enemy'
But I tell you, love your enemies
Bless those who curse you
Do good to those who hate you
And pray for those who mistreat you and persecute you.

Matthew 5:43-44

I believe, however, that God hasn't abandoned either group and that his plan hasn't changed. We were meant to work together, to collaborate, to communicate, to cooperate, and to reconcile. This is prefigured in the story of Isaac and Ishmael who after being separated when Ishmael was sent off to the East, came back together to bury their father, Abraham.

Abraham gave up the spirit
And died in a good old age
An old man, and full of years
And was gathered to his people.
Isaac and Ishmael, his sons
Buried him in the cave of Machpelah,

Genesis 25:8-9

I am convinced that this is the last work of God on this planet, the final reconciliation of two great religious heritages descended from the sons of Abraham. This great reunion is predicted by the prophet Isaiah and one thing we can be sure of, the God of Abraham is faithful to his promises.

Epilogue

"Arise, shine; for your light has come
And the glory of Jehovah is risen on you
For, behold, darkness shall cover the earth
And gross darkness the peoples
But Jehovah will arise on you
And his glory shall be seen on you...
Lift up your eyes all around, and see...
Your sons shall come from far...
Then you shall see and be radiant
And your heart shall thrill and be enlarged...
The multitude of camels shall cover you
The dromedaries of Midian and Ephah
All they from Sheba shall come
They shall bring gold and frankincense
And shall proclaim the praises of Jehovah.
All the flocks of Kedar shall be gathered together to you
The rams of Nebaioth shall minister to you
They shall come up with acceptance on my altar
And I will glorify the house of my glory.

Isaiah 60:1-7

To God belongs the East and the West;
And wheresoever you turn,
There is the Presence of God.
For God is omnipresent and omniscient.

Qur'an 2:115

The Bible relates the story of the Children of the East from their origins as the firstborn son of Abraham through their role in the Old Testament in bringing the sons of Isaac back to the worship of the true God all the way to the Messiah and the birth of Christianity to the rise of Islam and the end of the world.

Isaiah the prophet predicts that the Children of the East, as represented by the Muslims, will be a part of God's last day people.

In that day, there will be an altar to Jehovah
In the midst of the land of Egypt
And a pillar to Jehovah at its border.
It will be for a sign and for a witness
To Jehovah of Armies in the land of Egypt
For they will cry to Jehovah because of oppressors
And he will send them a savior and a defender
And he will deliver them.

Jehovah will be known to Egypt
And the Egyptians will know Jehovah in that day
Yes, they will worship...
And will vow a vow to Jehovah, and will perform it
Jehovah will strike Egypt, striking and healing
They will return to Jehovah
And he will be entreated by them
And will heal them

In that day there will be a highway
Out of Egypt to Assyria
And the Assyrian shall come into Egypt
And the Egyptian into Assyria
And the Egyptians will worship with the Assyrians.

In that day, Israel will be the third
With Egypt and with Assyria
A blessing in the midst of the earth
Because Jehovah of Armies has blessed them, saying
'Blessed be Egypt my people
Assyria the work of my hands
And Israel my inheritance.'

Isaiah 19:19-25

Both Egypt and Assyria are today Muslim lands, but God has promised them a reconciliation with spiritual Israel, the true believers among the Children of Isaac. Both lines will worship together and be a blessing on the road to salvation.

In Isaiah 60:1-6, the Bible talks about the end of the world when God's people will assemble and he will bring back his sons from far away. Who are these sons? They come on camels from Midian, Ephah and Sheba, or they have flocks from Kedar or Nebaioth. All are tribes of the Children of the East. They arrive bearing the riches of the Arab lands, gold and incense, and proclaiming God's praise. They are Muslims.

Finally, Isaiah prefigures heaven and those who will be there. Once again, joining the children of Isaac are the Children of the East coming on horses, mules and camels to worship God together throughout eternity.

The time comes, that I will gather all nations and languages
And they shall come, and shall see my glory.
I will set a sign among them...
Who have not heard my fame, neither have seen my glory
And they shall declare my glory among the nations.

They shall bring all your brothers
Out of all the nations for an offering to Jehovah
On horses,...on mules, and on dromedaries
To my holy mountain Jerusalem...
As the children of Israel bring their offering
In a clean vessel into the house of Jehovah
Of them also will I take for priests...

For as the new heavens and the new earth
Which I will make, shall remain before me...
So your seed and your name shall remain
It shall happen, that from one new moon to another
And from one Sabbath to another
Shall all flesh come to worship before me, says Jehovah

Isaiah 66:18-23

Genealogies

Abraham's Family Tree

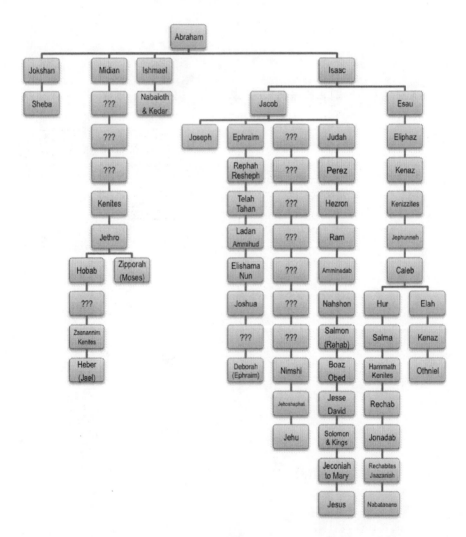

Terah's Family Tree

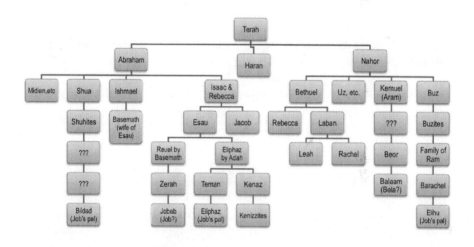

Genealogy of Muhammad

Although the Qur'an itself does not have any genealogies, the oldest extant biography of Muhammad, compiled 770-775 AD by Mohammed Ibn Ishak, and edited by Abu Muhammad Abd el Malik Ibn Hisham, opens:

Muhammad was the son of Abd Allah, son of Abd-ul-Muttalib, son of Hashim, son of Abdu Manaf, son of Qusay, son of Kilab, son of Hakeem, son of Kaab, son of Luayy, son of Ghalib, son of Fihr, son of Malik, son of Qays, son of Kinanah, son of Khuzaymah, son of Mudrikah, son of Ilyas, son of Mudhar, son of Nizar, son of Maad, son of Adnan, son of Udd, son of Muqawwam, son of Nakhour, son of Tahir, son of Yarub, son of Yashyub,

Son of Nabit (Nabaioth), son of Ismail (Ishmael), son of Ibrahim (Abraham), the Friend of God, son of Tarikh (Terah), son of Nakhour (Nahor), son of Sarukh (Serug), son of Rau (Reu), son of Falih (Peleg), son of Hud (Eber), son of Salih (Shelah), son of Arphakhshad (Arphaxad), son of Sham (Shem), son of Nuh (Noah), son of Lamekh (Lamech), son of Matushalakh (Methuselah), son of Akhanukh (Enoch), son of Aded (Jared), son of Mahlaleel (Mahalalel), son of Kaynan (Kenan), son of Anoush (Enosh), son of Shays (Seth), son of Adam, to whom may God be gracious!

Biblical names in ( ) from 1 Chronicles 1:1-4, 24-29:
Adam, Seth, Enosh, Kenan, Mahalalel, Jared, Enoch, Methuselah, Lamech, Noah,...Shem, Arphaxad, Shelah, Eber, Peleg, Reu, Serug, Nahor, Terah and Abram (the same is Abraham). The sons of Abraham: Isaac and Ishmael...the firstborn of Ishmael, Nabaioth.

Bibliography

Balaam (Bela?) son of Beor:
    King of Edom?: Genesis 36:32; 1 Chronicles 1:43
    From Aram Naharaim (Edom?): Deuteronomy 23:4; Genesis 24:10;
        Psalm 60:1 (preface)
    Numbers 22-24, 25:1-5; 31:8, 16; Deuteronomy 23:4-5;
        Joshua 13:22; 24:9-10; Nehemiah 13:2; Micah 6:5; 2 Peter 2:15;
        Jude 1:11; Revelation 2:14
    http://en.wikipedia.org/wiki/Balaam
Barak: Judges 4:6
Caleb (son of Jephunneh): Exodus 34:6-6; Numbers 13:6, 30; 14:6, 24, 30,
    38; 26:65; 32:12; 34:19; Deuteronomy 1:36; Joshua 14:6, 13-14;
    15:13-19 (daughter Acsah); 21:12; Judges 1:12-15 (daughter Acsah);
    1Samuel 25:3, 30:14; I Chronicles 4:15
    http://en.wikipedia.org/wiki/Caleb
Caleb (son of Hezron): 1 Chronicles 2:9, 17-19, 24, 42, 48-49 (daughter
    Acsah); 1 Chronicles 4:1
    New International Bible Dictionary, Douglas & Tenney, p 565
Hagar: Genesis 16:1-16; 21:8-20;
    http://en.wikipedia.org/wiki/Hagar_(Bible)
Heber the Kenite: Numbers 10:29-36; Judges 1:16, 4:11, 17, 21; 5:24
    New International Bible Dictionary, Douglas & Tenney, p 564-5
Hobab, Moses' brother-in-law: Numbers 10:29-32; Judges 1:16, 4:11
    New International Bible Dictionary, Douglas & Tenney, p 564-5
Ishmael: Genesis 16:1-16; 17:18-27; 21:8-20; 25:9, 12-18; I Chronicles
    1:28-29 Qur'an 2:125-140; Qur'an 6:86; Qur'an 19:54-55; Qur'an
    21:85; Qur'an 38:48
    http://en.wikipedia.org/wiki/Ishmael
Jael: 4:17-22; 5:24
    http://en.wikipedia.org/wiki/Jael

Jehu: 1 Kings 18-19, 21; 2 Kings 2, 4-10, 15:12; 2 Chronicles 22:7-9;
    Hosea 1:4
    http://en.wikipedia.org/wiki/Jehu
Jethro (Reuel): Exodus 2:18, 3:1, 4:18, 18:1-27; Numbers 10:29;
    http://en.wikipedia.org/wiki/Jethro_(Bible)
Job (Jobab?): Genesis 36:2-4, 10-17; 1 Chronicles 1:35, 37, 44-45;
    Job 1-42; Ezekiel 14:14, 20; James 5:11
    Qur'an 4:163; Qur'an 6:84; Qur'an 21:83-84; Qur'an 38:41-44
Job's Friends:
    Elihu: Genesis 22:20-22; Job 32:2, 6
    Eliphaz the Temanite: Genesis 36; Job 2:11, 4:1, 15:1, 22:1, 42:7,9
    Bildad the Shuite: Genesis 25:1-3; Job 2:11, 8:1, 18:1, 25:1, 42:9
Jonadab (Jehonadab) son of Rechab: 1 Chronicles 2:19, 50-51, 54-55;
    2 Kings 10:15, 23; Jeremiah 35
Joseph: Genesis 37, 39-50; Qur'an 12 (Yusuf)
Moses: Exodus 2-18, Numbers 10:29-32
Othniel: 1 Chronicles 4:13, 15; Joshua 15:17-18; Judges 1:13-14; 3:9-11
Rechabites: 1 Samuel 15:6; 2 Samuel 4:1-12; 2 Kings 25:1-26; 1
    Chronicles 2:55; Jeremiah 35, 39-40; 2 Corinthians 11:32-33
    New International Bible Dictionary, Douglas & Tenney, p 848-9
    http://en.wikipedia.org/wiki/Rechabites
    http://en.wikipedia.org/wiki/Hanif
    http://en.wikipedia.org/wiki/Aretas_IV_Philopatris
    Easton's Bible Dictionary, 1987, *Rechabites*
Revelation: Revelation 8:13, 9:1-21, 11:14-14, 14:7, 20:1-2
    The Great Controversy by Ellen G. White, chapter 11
    Millerite Signs of the Times, February 01, 1840, by Josiah Litch
    The History of the Decline and Fall of the Roman Empire by Edward
        Gibbon. Chap. LXIV page 1119
Saul: Judges 1:36; 2 Kings 14:7; Isaiah 16:1; Jeremiah 35, 40:8; Acts 9:1-
    25; 18:3; 2 Corinthians 11:30-33; Galatians 1:13-20
    Qur'an 7:73-79; Qur'an 11:61-68; Qur'an 26:141-159
    The Catholic Encyclopedia, Vol. 1, ed. by Charles Herbermann, p. 667
    New International Bible Dictionary, Douglas & Tenney, p 775-6
    (Petra), 912-3 (Seir, Sela)
    http://en.wikipedia.org/wiki/Paul_the_Apostle
    http://en.wikipedia.org/wiki/Aretas_IV_Philopatris
    http://en.wikipedia.org/wiki/Nabataeans
Terah/Nahor/Laban: Genesis 11:27-32; 22:20-23; 24:15, 24, 47; 29:1-30
Wise Men: Matthew 2; Luke 2
    http://en.wikipedia.org/wiki/Magi
    http://en.wikipedia.org/wiki/Biblical_Magi

About the Author

James Appel, MD holds a Bachelor of Arts in Theology from Southern Adventist University and a Doctor of Medicine from the Loma Linda University School of Medicine. He completed a three year residency in Family Practice at the Ventura County Medical Center in California. He has spent the last seven years as the only doctor at the Béré Adventist Hospital directly responsible for the health care of over 150,000 Chadians. It was in Chad that he was introduced to Islam and began studying the Qur'an and other books on Muslims. Coming from a long line of Christian Ministers and Missionaries, Dr. Appel grew up in an environment where thinking about and debating spirituality and religion was part of the family heritage. His Danish wife, Sarah, has just given birth to twins...one is named David.

Made in the USA
Charleston, SC
26 March 2012